RUMORS OF INJUSTICE

The Cases of
Ilse Koch and Rudolph Spanner

George R. Mastroianni

George R. Mastroianni

Copyright © 2021

All Rights Reserved

Cover and interior design by David Ter-Avanesyan/Ter33Design

Note on photos: Many of the photos in this paper are quite old and are quite widely available on many internet websites and in books. Unless otherwise noted, all photos in this paper are believed to be in the public domain. Many are assumed to be at the United States National Archives and Records Administration. If notified that any of these photos are subject to copyright, they will be immediately removed pending the receipt of appropriate permission.

The author is indebted to David Frey, Tomaz Jardim, Avi Lowenstein, Connor Sebestyen, and Kathleen O'Donnell for helpful comments on an earlier version of this manuscript. Any errors are the sole responsibility of the author.

Other works by George Mastroianni

Mastroianni, G., Palmer, B., Penetar, D., and Tepe, V. (Eds.) (2011). *A Warrior's Guide to Psychology and Performance.* Herndon, Va: Potomac Books.

Mastroianni, G.R. (2018). *Of Mind and Murder: Toward a More Comprehensive Psychology of the Holocaust.* New York: Oxford University Press.

Mastroianni, G.R. (2020). *Misremembering the Holocaust: The Liberation of Buchenwald and the Limits of Memory.* Colorado Springs: George Mastroianni.

CONTENTS

THE STUDY OF RUMORS IN WWII AND AFTER..................8

FROM WAR'S END TO THE IMT: ILSE KOCH...................14

FROM WAR'S END TO THE IMT: RUDOLF SPANNER..............29

AFTER NUREMBERG: ILSE KOCH.............................36

AFTER NUREMBERG: THE OUTCOME FOR RUDOLPH SPANNER.......56

THE POWER OF RUMOR.....................................59

THE LAMPSHADE..75

BEAST OF BUCHENWALD?..................................100

Figure 1. Ilse and Karl Otto Koch. This photo was taken in 1936, before the Kochs were posted to Buchenwald. The boy is Manfred, Karl Koch's son from his first marriage. From the Koch photo album in the collection of the National Archives and Records Administration (NARA). The photo was found at https://forum.axishistory.com/viewtopic.php?t=139601&start=30.

RUMORS OF INJUSTICE:
THE CASES OF ILSE KOCH AND RUDOLF SPANNER

Long before the telegraph, radio, or television, let alone the internet or "social media", the seeming advantage in ease of transmission enjoyed by falsehood over truth was eloquently noted by Jonathan Swift in 1710:

"Besides, as the vilest Writer has his Readers, so the greatest Liar has his Believers; and it often happens, that if a Lie be believ'd only for an Hour, it has done its Work, and there is no farther occasion for it. Falsehood flies, and the Truth comes limping after it; so that when Men come to be undeceiv'd, it is too late; the Jest is over, and the Tale has had its Effect..."[1]

A common species of falsehood is the rumor. One definition of a rumor is "A specific (or topical) proposition for belief, passed along from person to person, usually by word of mouth, without secure standards of evidence being present."[2]

That rumors can have dramatic consequences in the lives of individuals is illustrated by two cases which have interesting similarities, and important differences: those of Ilse Koch and Rudolph Spanner. Ilse Koch, wife of the first Commandant of Buchenwald, was rumored to have selected prisoners with tattoos that struck her fancy, caused them to be murdered, and then made or had made decorative objects, such as lampshades, purses, and book covers, from their tattooed skin. Rudolph Spanner, a physician who worked at a medical school in Danzig, Poland, was rumored to have had prisoners from the nearby Stutthof concentration camp murdered and had their bodies brought to his facility, where he rendered them into soap.

The rumors about Ilse Koch flew around the world in the summer and fall of 1945; the rumors about Rudolph Spanner took wing in Poland at the same time. These rumors would become objects of testimony at the International Military Tribunal (IMT) at Nuremberg in December 1945 and January 1946, though neither Ilse Koch nor Rudolph Spanner was charged with any crime. While these two cases seemingly were characterized by many similarities, they ended very differently for the two individuals. The rumors about Ilse Koch and Rudolph Spanner probably arose through similar mechanisms, but were ultimately treated very differently by legal and judicial authorities, by the press, and by the public.

THE STUDY OF RUMORS IN WWII AND AFTER

We humans create and pass along rumors, and we probably started creating them and passing them along very early in our history. This enduring feature of human social interaction was of immense concern to American military and government authorities in the first few years of WWII. There was deep concern about the effects of rumors on morale, both in the military forces and on the home front. Authorities saw rumors that negatively affected morale as potential threats to recruiting, war production, and compliance with wartime rules and regulations. Rumors were also a matter of significant concern to the Nazi authorities in wartime Germany.[3] The Nazis were sensitive to public opinion, and especially to rumors that might undermine morale or reduce support for the regime.

Gordon Allport, a social psychologist who was active in organizing American psychologists in support of the war effort, became intensely interested in rumors and in finding ways to eliminate them and their potentially destructive effects from the public square. Allport and his graduate student, Robert Knapp, helped establish and operate "rumor clinics" that were intended to stop rumors by exposing and debunking them: rumors were collected and printed in newspapers weekly, along with a refutation and often, some psychological analysis of the rumor's origin and apparent social function.[4]

Allport and Leo Postman produced a book-length treatment of rumor (*The Psychology of Rumor*) shortly after WWII.[5] Allport and Postman sketched a theory of the origin, evolution, and transmission of rumors that has remained very influential. According to Allport and Postman, "Rumor travels when events have importance in the lives of individuals and when the news received about them is either lacking or subjectively ambiguous."[6] Rumors survive in societies because they are repeated by people, and people only bother to repeat rumors that are relevant or interesting to them. What makes rumors relevant or interesting? Allport and Postman adopted a somewhat Freudian interpretation of the motivations behind most rumors:

> "...rumors often assuage immediate emotional tension by providing a verbal outlet that gives relief; they often protect and justify the existence of these emotions which, if faced directly, might be unacceptable to their possessor; they sometimes provide a broader interpretation of various puzzling features of the environment, and so play a prominent part in the intellectual drive to render the surrounding world intelligible."[7]

Motivation is not enough to sustain a rumor, however. There must also be uncertainty or ambiguity: "The ambiguity may arise from the fact that the news is not clearly reported, or from the fact that conflicting versions of the news have reached the individual, or from his incapacity to comprehend the news he receives."[8] Once rumors arise, they are subject to the processes of leveling,[9] sharpening,[10] and assimilation,[11] according to Allport and Postman.

Figure 2. *Gordon Allport studied rumors from an academic perspective, but also tried to combat rumors during WWII using "rumor clinics."*

Levelling is a loss of detail in a rumor, while sharpening is the selection and accentuation of certain details. Assimilation occurs as rumors are affected by an individual's biases, beliefs, or desires. While these theoretical ideas of Allport and Postman are still influential, others have addressed the psychology and sociology of rumor, as well. Ralph Rosnow[12] offered revisions to some ideas of Allport and Postman, and Tamotsu Shibutani's analysis of rumor[13] added a sociological perspective.

RUMORS IN THE CAMPS

Based on the conditions posited by Allport and Postman as rumor-genic, it would be difficult to think of an environment better suited to the creation and transmission of rumors than Nazi concentration camps. Survivors often use words such as violent, unpredictable, capricious, arbitrary, and dangerous to describe life in the camps. Many acknowledge that luck played a significant role, perhaps a dominant role, in determining their fate. The only information available to prisoners was that which the camp administrators chose to deliver, or that which could be gleaned informally from guards and other prisoners. Prospects for success in the daily struggle for survival could be augmented by learning as much as possible as quickly as possible about how to behave, who to avoid, where and how to obtain the necessities of life, how to get the best work detail, and so on. Life itself might depend on information gained this way: what could be more important? And to describe the camp environment as characterized by uncertainty and ambiguity for prisoners is to traffic in understatement.

I suspect that it was quite difficult for prisoners to sort out truth from falsehood or exaggeration in the moment, and, perhaps paradoxically, sometimes became yet more so when recalling their experiences years or decades later. Some survivor testimonies contain inaccuracies. Some do not. Some of the inaccuracies arise simply from the normal operations of human memory: these events happened long ago, conditions at the time often did not favor laying down strong memories, and the past few decades have filled the public square with Holocaust-related information that might now be mistaken as a personal memory. While we tend to privilege survivor testimonies because of our respect for survivors, their memories are not necessarily any more accurate than anyone else's.

STUDIES OF HOLOCAUST-RELATED RUMORS

The rumor-genic conditions of importance and uncertainty also existed for Jews under or about to fall under Nazi control in the years and months leading up to the Holocaust. The Nazi monopoly over official public information, coupled with the dynamic and unpredictable developments in Nazi Jewish policy during the Third Reich, can only have encouraged an intense rumor culture in Jewish communities subject to or threatened by Nazi rule. Amos Goldberg [14] studied the culture of rumors in the Warsaw Ghetto. Goldberg's detailed history of the origins, functions, and evolution of rumors in the ghetto offer a fascinating look at the role rumors played in community life. It seems likely that similar social processes were unfolding in Jewish communities large and small as the Nazis consolidated power and turned their attention increasingly to the "Jewish problem", especially after Kristallnacht in 1938, when the position of Jews threatened by Nazi rule became ever more precarious.

Jovan Byford and Maris Rowe-McCulloch have made seminal contributions to our understanding of the mechanisms of rumor development and transmission in the Holocaust. Rowe-McCulloch's analysis of a specific and localized rumor, [15] that children in Rostov-on-Don were murdered by the Nazis' application of a topical poison smeared on their lips, knits together a fact pattern that at the time was known only incompletely. The persistent rumors that children were killed by having a poisonous black substance applied to their lips most likely arose as a result of the appearance of the bodies of children who were murdered in gas vans. Rowe-McCulloch makes a persuasive case that this rumor arose under conditions of importance and uncertainty as posited by Allport and Postman, and then maintained and perpetuated by social and institutional networks.

Jovan Byford's fascinating study of rumors of gas vans used by the Nazis to murder Yugoslav prisoners (non-Jews) at the Banjica camp in Belgrade, Yugoslavia [16] traces the origin of these stories to the earlier, actual use of gas vans to murder Jews at the Semlin camp in the same city. Byford shows how a very few confused and contradictory testimonies can become the basis for an enduring legend. By carefully following the chronology of the evolution of this rumor, Byford shows how these problematic testimonies were cloaked in credibility by official institutions far more interested in perpetuating stories deemed to be socially and politically favorable than in rigorously assessing the truth of these stories. Byford's analysis hints at a two-stage life-cycle for some rumors. Many rumors arise and then disappear, but some become integrated into longer-term narratives because they serve social and political ends, a process that dovetails neatly with Maurice Halbwach's conception of collective or social memory. [17] These two distinct processes are especially important in the cases of Ilse Koch and Rudolph Spanner: the rumors about Ilse Koch were, as we shall see, integrated into social and political narratives far more effectively and extensively than were the rumors about Rudolph Spanner.

FROM WAR'S END TO THE IMT: ILSE KOCH

For those unfamiliar with the story of Ilse Koch, reiteration of a few biographical facts will help frame discussion of the rumors about her.[18] Born Margarete Ilse Kohler in Dresden in 1906, she was an accounting clerk who joined the Nazi Party in 1932, when female membership was still quite low. She married Colonel [19] Karl Otto Koch, an SS officer who had extensive experience running Nazi concentration camps, in 1937. Koch was posted to Buchenwald in 1938, where he served as the first Commandant of the camp. Ilse Koch became an enthusiastic equestrian at a riding school in the nearby town of Weimar early in her husband's tenure at Buchenwald, and the Kochs had an indoor riding ring built for her at the camp, reportedly at great expense using money stolen from prisoners and in prisoner labor and suffering. Ilse Koch's children were all born while she was at Buchenwald, in 1938, 1939, and 1940, save one, who was born in 1947 while she was in American custody after the war.

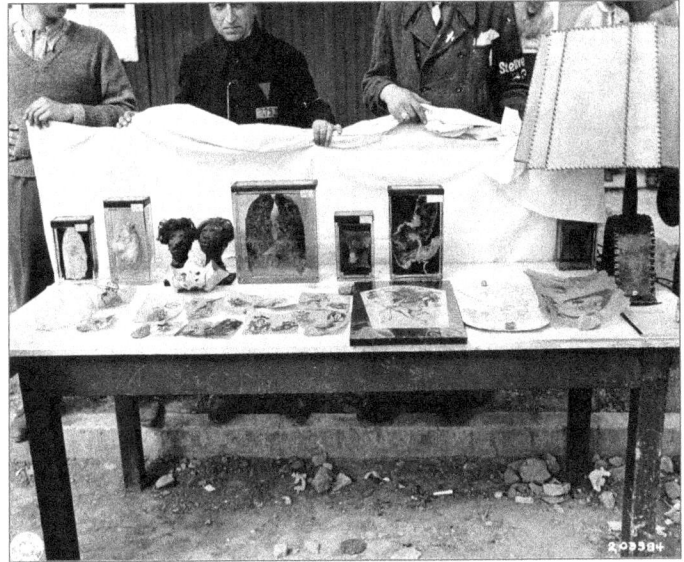

Figure 3. German civilians from the nearby town of Weimar were brought to visit Buchenwald on April 16, 1945. They were marched by this exhibit table, upon which is the alleged human-skin lampshade. United States Holocaust Memorial Museum Photograph 74066.

RUMORS ABOUT ILSE KOCH ARE PUBLICIZED

Buchenwald was liberated on Wednesday, April 11, 1945 by American troops of the United States Third Army. General George S. Patton, Third Army Commander, visited Buchenwald on Sunday, April 15 (he had also visited Ohrdruf, a sub-camp of Buchenwald, a few days earlier with Eisenhower) and issued orders for the population of nearby Weimar to be brought to the camp to see for themselves the horrors that had taken place just a few miles from their homes. This was done on Monday, April 16, 1945.

The visit of Weimar civilians was extensively covered by international media, and photos and newsreels quickly brought images of the event to the world. A table containing a lampshade said to have been made of human skin, a shrunken head, and other anatomical objects was prominently displayed, and was understandably given especially wide circulation in the media. Print media and newsreels showing images of these objects drew worldwide attention. Evidence of such monstrous crimes naturally generated intense interest in identifying those responsible. A page-1 story in the April 20 edition of the *Metropolitan Pasadena Star-News* mentioned the lampshades and tanned pieces of human skin;[20] an article on page 4 of the *Mexia City Herald*, Mexia, Texas, datelined April 21 at Buchenwald by Ann Stringer quoted a "Dutch engineer" who had been a former prisoner. This article states that human skin lampshades had been made on the orders of the Commandant's wife, and that she had inmates killed in order to harvest their tattoos.[21] The basic elements of the rumors that would dog Ilse Koch were thus in the news a mere fortnight after the liberation of the camp.

These rumors were clearly widespread in the camp at the time of liberation. A group of American officers who visited Buchenwald on April 16, 1945, filed a report on April 25 entitled, "Inspection of German Concentration Camp for Political Prisoners Located at Buchenwald on the North Edge of Weimar". The report included the following passage:

> "The 20 April Paris edition of the Stars and Stripes carried on page 2 a story regarding the use, by the SS officers of the camp, of tattooed human skin for souvenirs. This story is true in every respect. Commandant L'Hopital stated that the wife of one of the SS officers started the fad; that any prisoner who

happened to have extensive tattooing of any sort on his body was brought to her; that if she found the tattooing satisfactory the prisoner was killed and skinned; that the skin with the tattooing was then tanned and made into souvenirs such as lamp shades, wall pictures, book ends, etc; that about 40 examples of this artistry were found in the SS offices and quarters in the camp. This statement was confirmed by 1st Lt. Walter F. Emmons. And we ourselves saw 6 examples at Camp HQ, including a lampshade." [22]

Commandant Rene L'Hopital was a high-ranking French officer who was acquainted with many well-known Americans, including the late Theodore Roosevelt, Jr, and Admiral Byrd. L'Hopital accompanied the group of officers at Buchenwald on April 16, and his authority lent weight to the tattoo story, though he had been at Buchenwald for only two months before his release, and could not have had any direct knowledge of the alleged events.

Some did at least attempt to separate fact from rumor: an article by M.E. Walter, writing for the Associated Press, offered a more cautious assessment in an April 30, 1945 piece: "Human skin was tanned and used for lampshades and other ornaments, it was said. Whether this is true or not we cannot say from personal knowledge, but we did see large sections of tanned human skin, easily recognizable. Nearby was a wire frame for a lampshade."

Figure 4. The human-skin evidence presented at the IMT: three pieces of tanned skin with tattoos. A shrunken head may also be seen on the table to the left. United States Holocaust Memorial Museum Photograph 10407

TESTIMONY AT NUREMBERG ABOUT ILSE KOCH

Newsreels and newspapers reported the rumors about Ilse Koch and her role in the procurement of tattooed skin and the making of lampshades from these materials throughout the summer and fall of 1945. These stories were brought to a new level of public awareness when testimony regarding human skin lampshades and Ilse Koch was introduced at the IMT. A story datelined December 13, 1945 from Nuremberg and printed in many newspapers (including the Des Moines Tribune, which ran the story on page 1) included this statement: "The three pieces of human skin

Figure 5. It is difficult to tell from the photographs, but none of these three specimens obviously matches any of the items seen on the table at Buchenwald. Many news stories reported that they were pieces of lampshades, though there was no evidence of this. United States Holocaust Memorial Museum Photograph 10407 (detail)

tanned into parchment for lampshades for the wife of SS *Standartenfuehrer* Koch came from victims at Buchenwald, according to an affidavit by a former camp inmate." The headline of this story was, "Nazis View Human Skin Lampshades: Exhibits from Torture Camps".[24] The source of this allegation against Ilse Koch was a former inmate of Buchenwald named Andreas Pfaffenberger. Pfaffenberger was a German citizen arrested for making uncomplimentary statements about local Nazi officials. He was brought to Buchenwald in 1938 and was released from Buchenwald to serve in the Wehrmacht in June 1944. He was captured by American troops a short time later, on November 2, 1944. Pfaffenberger provided testimony that included rumors about Ilse Koch's conduct. The document introduced at Nuremberg was published in a PW (Prisoner of War) Bulletin dated December 19, 1944. [25] This document appears to be a verbatim transcript of an interview with Pfaffenberger, written in the first person, though the interview may have taken place before the publication date of the extract. The December 19, 1944 statement by Pfaffenberger presented at Nuremberg mentions the human skin lampshades:

> "In 1939, all prisoners with tattooing on them were ordered to report to the dispensary. No one knew what the purpose was. But after the tattooed prisoners had been examined, the ones with the best and most artistic specimens were kept in the dispensary, and then killed by injections, administered by KARL BEIGS, a criminal prisoner. The corpses were then turned over to the pathological department, where the desired pieces of tattooed skin were detached from the bodies and treated. The finished products were turned over to SS Standartenfuehrer KOCH's wife, who had them fashioned into lampshades and other ornamental household articles. I myself saw such tattoed [sic] skins with various designs and legends on them, such as "Hans'l und Gret'l", which one prisoner had had on his knee, and ships from prisoners' chests. This work was done by a prisoner named WERNERBACH." [26]

Lawyers representing Ernst Kaltenbrunner and Martin Bormann, who were defendants at Nuremberg (though Bormann was being tried in absentia) objected to this testimony and moved to have it struck from the record, a motion which was denied. Because the testimony had been challenged, though, a search was begun to locate Pfaffenberger and bring him to Nuremberg to provide additional evidence. This was accomplished and Pfaffenberger was interviewed by Thomas J. Dodd and First Lieutenant Daniel F. Margolies on February 1, 1946, at Nuremberg.[27]

Figure 6. Thomas J. Dodd at Nuremberg. United States Holocaust Memorial Museum Photograph 16780. From the Lorenz Schmuhl Collection.

This interview was remarkable on at least two counts. First, despite persistent and specific questioning, Pfaffenberger could not directly connect a tattoo he had seen on a living prisoner to Ilse Koch and to a lampshade. Second, Pfaffenberger claimed that people in Weimar must have known about the objects made from human skin because of the arrests of Waldemar Hoven, Hermann Florstedt, Martin Sommer[28] and Ilse Koch by the SS in August 1943. This inference of Pfaffenberger's may help explain an important step in the development of the rumors about Ilse Koch, a point to which we shall return.

THE SS TRIAL OF THE KOCHS

The American legal authorities enlisted to track down Pfaffenberger suggested to Thomas Dodd that he also consider the testimony of Dr. Georg Konrad Morgen, a former SS judge.[29] Morgen had investigated and prosecuted the Kochs in 1943-1944. Karl Otto Koch had run afoul of Josias Erbprinz zu Waldeck und Pyrmont,[30] the Higher SS and Police Leader in Kassel, under whose jurisdiction Buchenwald lay. Koch had had three prisoners, medical orderlies who had treated him for syphilis apparently contracted on an excursion to Norway, murdered, apparently to prevent them ever telling what they knew about his disease. One of these men was known to Waldeck, as he had successfully treated him for a medical condition. Waldeck's investigations of the prisoner murders, along with Koch's audaciously larcenous management of Buchenwald and diversion of funds to his personal use, led to his arrest in December 1941 and subsequent transfer to Majdanek in early 1942. SS Colonel Hermann Pister[31] was appointed Commandant of Buchenwald in Koch's place in December 1941.

Majdanek[32] was originally intended to acquire the very dubious distinction of becoming the largest Nazi concentration camp, and Koch's appointment as Commandant was a potential road to rehabilitation, so his goose was far from cooked at this point. Ilse Koch remained at Buchenwald while her husband assumed his new post in Poland. From early 1942 until August 1943, Ilse Koch lived with her children in the Commandant's villa at Buchenwald, but the camp was commanded during this time by Hermann Pister, Karl Otto Koch's successor. A dramatic escape of Russian prisoners at Majdanek in July 1942 [33] tarnished Koch's star, though, and in August of that year he was demoted to the ignominious position of command of a postal unit. His name attracted attention anew when a corruption investigation at Buchenwald involving a man named Bornschein implicated Koch, and Konrad Morgen re-enters the story here as the SS Judge assigned to investigate the Kochs.[35]

Figure 7. Hermann Pister, Karl Otto Koch's successor as Commandant of Buchenwald. United States Holocaust Memorial Museum Photograph 23662. From the Lorenz Schmuhl Collection.

The Kochs were arrested by the SS on August 24, 1943, at Buchenwald and were imprisoned in Weimar. They remained in custody for approximately a year, until they were formally tried by the SS court in late 1944. Karl Otto Koch was convicted and sentenced to death; Ilse Koch was acquitted of the charges that had been levelled against her (receiving stolen property) and moved to Ludwigsburg. Karl Otto Koch remained in custody until his execution by firing squad on the orders of Waldeck on April 5, 1945 at Buchenwald, six days before the liberation of the camp.

In late 1945, as the lurid and sensational charges regarding tattooed human skin presented at Nuremberg were widely spread in newspapers and in films, American interrogators were naturally interested in whether Morgen had sought or uncovered any evidence that Ilse Koch had been involved in such practices during his investigation of the Kochs in 1943 and 1944. In early 1946, after the evidence against Ilse Koch had been presented at Nuremberg and had been challenged by defense attorneys for Kaltenbrunner and Bormann, American authorities questioned Morgen. Morgen told American authorities that his investigation of the Kochs was not related to the sensational charges that had been raised against Ilse Koch:

> "Subject of the charge and the sentence of KOCH were the accusation of continued embezzlement and particularly serious unfaithfulness qualifying him as a public enemy, of continued serious military disobedience consisting in running the concentration camps Buchenwald and Lublin contrary to orders given to him and all morale [sic] codes; furthermore of murder of the inmates KRAEMER, PEIX, and WENDEL. The charge sheet including explanations I have kept since the trial and submitted to the American investigating authorities. Not subject of the trial was the tanning of human skin as well as the alleged processing of the latter into lamp shades and other utility products, this being mentioned at the Nuremberg trials at this time. At the time I had subjected with the aid of a plain clothesman, the home of KOCH and his wife to a very accurate official surprise search. No such objects were found at this occasion. I consider it impossible that such objects would have escaped our attention if they had been there." [36]

Morgen described the anatomical-pathological work at Buchenwald involving human skin as scientifically respectable,[37] serving as a source of specimens for academic and research institutions in Germany. He claimed that the novel contribution of Buchenwald to this scientific enterprise was the tanning of the specimens, rather than their preservation in a liquid solution. The latter method caused tattoos to fade, whereas the former preserved them more vividly and permanently. On the specific claims that prisoners were deliberately killed only for the purpose of obtaining their tattooed skin, Morgen went on to say:

Figure 8. SS Judge Dr. Konrad Morgen. From the Archive of the Fritz Bauer Institute, Konrad Morgen Estate. https://jungle.world/artikel/2017/26/sein-gewissen-versagte-nicht-gaenzlich.

"SS-Standartenfuehrer KOCH had brought to his office, which was open to only a few persons, some of these anatomical specimens. These were the prepared head of a hanged murderer and a lamp shade made out of human skin. SS-Standartenfuehrer PISTER, the successor of KOCH, left these objects in their places. It is my impression that he did this in order to illustrate the peculiar taste of his predecessor. In any case, that is what he said when he drew my attention to these objects. It is naturally not impossible that members of the pathological department of the concentration camp Buchenwald had also given respective private orders to the inmates employed there. However, it is not known to me that this actually was the

> case, nor that inmates were killed for the express purpose of obtaining skin. My attention would most certainly have been drawn to such a procedure by the inmates in form of a rumor. This never happened. I consider the statement now made to the contrary as highly improbable already because the daily death rate at Buchenwald was so high that scientific material was always available to excess." [38]

Konrad Morgen's testimony suggests that the rumors implicating Ilse Koch in the procurement of human skin for the purposes of making fetish items for herself arose sometime after her arrest in August 1943, or at least were not yet so widespread at that time that he became aware of them. By the time he made this statement (December 28, 1945—two weeks after Pfaffenberger's testimony had been introduced at Nuremberg) the rumors about Ilse Koch's role in the murder of prisoners were reported as fact in many news stories. Pfaffenberger had reported these rumors as early as November 2, 1944, when he was captured by the American Army, so they must have been current by then.

ORIGIN OF A RUMOR?

One function of rumors is to assist people in making sense of the world—by knitting seemingly unrelated facts and events into a coherent narrative. Rumors can help us formulate plausible explanations for events, and thereby achieve a greater sense of mastery over our environment. There were many facts at Buchenwald seemingly waiting to be knit into the

Ilse Koch narrative. Buchenwald had both a tannery and a bookbindery, for example, which employed prisoners as workers. Buchenwald was also equipped with craft workshops that produced high-quality decorative and commemorative objects for the personal use of SS officers. There was indeed a research program at Buchenwald involving tattooed human skin, undertaken by Dr. Erich Wagner, which produced a dissertation on the topic in 1940.[39] Wagner was interested in the possible association between tattoos and criminality, and studied some 800 prisoner tattoos at Buchenwald. It appears that SS Doctor Lolling, chief SS physician for the concentration camps, continued to secure specimens of tattooed skin and send these to academic and research institutions in Germany after Wagner's thesis had been completed.[40] And Ilse Koch did commit abuses against prisoners and incite others to do so. If Morgen is to be believed that rumors about Ilse Koch having prisoners murdered for their tattoos and having lampshades produced from their skin were not current at Buchenwald before the arrest of the Kochs in August 1943, it is nevertheless clear that such rumors were present by November of 1944, when Pfaffenberger was captured. It is conceivable that the rumors about Ilse Koch arose, or were amplified, elaborated, and given more credence, after she was arrested in August 1943, as prisoners

Figure 9. Erich Wagner's 1940 dissertation based on tattoos from Buchenwald: "A Contribution to Tattoo Questions".

sought to understand and explain these events. The human skin lampshade story may have been one way of explaining the fact of Ilse Koch's arrest (and those of Hoven, Florstedt, and Sommer) in August, 1943.

The story that Ilse Koch was having prisoners murdered to produce household and personal objects made of tattooed human skin plausibly integrates a host of potentially unrelated facts about Buchenwald. Once rumors arise, they are subject to levelling, sharpening, assimilation, and other psychological and social influences: perhaps this is how the rumors about Ilse Koch began, and were subsequently amplified, elaborated, homogenized, and eventually, converted into false memories of survivors. The rumors connecting Ilse Koch to human skin objects may not have been particularly widespread at Buchenwald prior to the Kochs' arrest or the liberation, though in later years many survivors would report that such rumors were a commonplace of camp lore. The *Buchenwald Report,* [41] which was produced by a group of prisoners that included Eugen Kogon, who would later incorporate the work into his book *Der SS-Staat. Das System der deutschen Konzentrationslager* [42] was compiled in the first few weeks after the liberation of the camp but had very little to say about human skin products. The few mentions of human skin lampshades in the report always connect them to Karl Koch, not Ilse Koch. The single mention of Ilse Koch in connection with human skin is from Kurt Titz (Dietz), a *kalfaktor* (household servant) in the Koch home [43] who claimed that she had a purse or handbag made of human skin of which she was very proud—at that time, no mention of lampshades was made.

FROM WAR'S END TO THE IMT: RUDOLF SPANNER

Rudolf Spanner was born in 1895 in Metternich bei Koblenz, Germany. Rudolf Spanner was a member of the Nazi Party, though a rather late joiner, and of several other Nazi organizations, but was not a member of the SA or SS. Spanner was nominated for the Nobel Prize in Physiology or Medicine in 1939 by Primo Dorello.[44] Dr. Spanner found himself working at the Danzig Anatomic Institute, a small organization associated with the medical school in Danzig (now Gdansk) during WWII.

There were rumors during World War II that Jews were exterminated and their bodies used to produce soap. This rumor circulated in Germany and in the world press as early as late 1942.[45] How and when the rumor originated is not known, but there had also been a rumor about Germans turning bodies into soap in World War I. In the earlier case, though, the rumor, which was widely circulated by the British, was that the German authorities used dead German soldiers to produce soap.[46]

During World War II, cakes of soap marked "RJF"[47] were produced and used in some German-occupied countries. These letters were inter-

Figure 10. Soap issued to Edward Graf while a prisoner at a Nazi concentration camp. (USHMM Collection)

preted by some as initializing "Rein judisches Fett", or "pure Jewish fat", indicating that this soap had been made from the corpses of murdered Jews. This rumor was quite widespread, and is still believed by some. Thoroughly investigated after the war, this rumor has been completely debunked and is recognized as false by most legitimate Holocaust scholars and institutions. The letters "RIF" apparently stood for "Reichstelle fuer industrielle Fettversorgung", or "Reich Office for Industrial Fat Supply".

In April and May of 1945, at the same time rumors about Ilse Koch and human-skin lampshades began to spread from Buchenwald, rumors about the activities of Rudolf Spanner were coalescing five hundred miles to the northeast, in Danzig. The role played by Andreas Pfaffenberger in the Ilse Koch case was played by a man named Zygmunt Mazur in the case of Rudolf Spanner. The Danzig Anatomic Institute was inspected by representatives of the Polish government [48] in mid-April, 1945, about

Figure 11. The "maceration" building at the Danzig Anatomic Institute, where Rudolph Spanner worked.

the same time as the liberation of Buchenwald. During these initial visits, of which no written record exists, inspectors saw examples of a "whitish or grayish mass, which former employees told them was 'soap' made from human fat."[49] On May 4, 1945, Russian and Polish officials visited the Institute and were given pieces of soap by a former employee. The soap was allegedly made from human fat by another former employee, who was identified to the visitor as Zygmunt Mazur. Mazur was arrested that very day.

On May 8, 1945, the day the Nazis surrendered, a Polish commission visited the Danzig Anatomic Institute and took photographs of the scene.[50] One of the visitors was Stanislaw Strabski, a Pole who had also visited the Institute on the 4th of May. Strabski immediately drafted an article for a Polish newspaper in which he reported that "discoveries at the Danzig Anatomic Institute had finally and irrefutably proven that the Germans had boiled their victims to soap, as had been rumored all over Europe during the war, but due to lack of evidence, could not be verified directly at the extermination sites."[51] On May 11, the Main Commission for the Investigation of German Crimes in Poland visited the site. Zygmunt Mazur was interrogated the next day, and was shown a recipe for the production of soap dated February 15, 1944, supposedly found at the Danzig Anatomic Institute. "Mazur confessed to making soap from human fat according to this recipe, and told details of the soap-making process."[52] According to Joachim Neander:

> "The findings of the Main Commission—that in the Anatomic Institute, under the direction of Professor Rudolf Spanner, soap was made from human fat for commercial use—were never questioned in Poland for more than 55 years. They guided all further action from the Polish side and found their way into literature, encyclopedias, and school textbooks."[53]

Two more Commissions visited the Institute on May 16/17 and May 18/19 1945, though neither mentioned soap made from human fat in their reports.[54] Zygmunt Mazur was interrogated by Soviet authorities on May 28, June 11, and June 12, 1945. Mazur stated that he had received the recipe for soap-making dated February 15, 1944 directly from Professor Spanner, that he had personally used soap made from this recipe for personal hygiene, and that his mother used the soap for laundering clothes. Mazur was presented to journalists in early July, and an article entitled "*The Human Soap Factory of Gdansk*", based on his reports, was published in an English-language newspaper on July 13, 1945.[55] Mazur died the next day, apparently of typhus.

The Americans presented their shrunken head and tattooed skin evidence related to Ilse Koch at Nuremberg on December 13, 1945. On February 19, 1946, Mazur's testimony from the Soviet interrogations in

May and June, 1945, was introduced by Soviet prosecutors at the International Military Tribunal at Nuremberg. Testimony of two former British prisoners of war of at least five who had worked at the Danzig Anatomic Institute was also presented. These two British POWs were employed as unskilled laborers, and testified that they had seen a substance removed from the tanks at the Institute, cut into blocks, and used for cleaning.[56] Neander suggests that the testimony of the British POWs was probably influenced by prosecutors:

> "A glance at the testimonies of the five British witnesses in chronological order reveals a "cumulative enrichment with soap": the later the witness testified, the more he told about "soap-making". This gives rise to the suspicion that the context of the interrogations influenced the memory of the witnesses. Undoubtedly the British and Soviet investigators closely cooperated in the Danzig soap case, and it is certainly no accident that the two "most enriched" British testimonies appeared as Soviet evidence at Nuremberg."[57]

The process suggested by Neander in the case of the testimony of these British POWs is called the misinformation effect by psychologists. Elizabeth Loftus, who pioneered ground breaking research into the accuracy of eyewitness testimony, has studied this phenomenon extensively, and has developed specific methods and procedures that interrogators and investigators can use to avoid contaminating testimony in this way.[58] Her work is fairly recent, and it is likely that the same kind of contamination suspected by Neander in the case of these British POWs was at work in some of the survivor testimony against Ilse Koch.

The Soviets also introduced physical evidence: two pieces of soap alleged to have been made from human fat, and interestingly, two pieces of a leather-like material the Soviets claimed was half-finished tanned human skin. According to the Soviet prosecutor:

> "I submit half-finished and some finished soap. (Exhibit USSR-393) Here you shall see a small piece of finished soap, which from the exterior, after lying about a few months, reminds you of ordinary household soap. I give it over to the Tribunal. Beside this I now submit to the Tribunal the samples of semi-tanned human skin (Exhibit I] USSR-394). The samples which I now submit prove that the process of manufacturing soap was already completely worked out by the Institute of Danzig; as to the skin it still looks like a semi-finished product. The skin which resembles most the leather used in manufacture is the one you see on top at the left. So one can consider that the experiments on the industrial fabrication of soap from human fats were quite completed in the Danzig Institute. Experiments on tanning of human skin were still incomplete and only the victorious advance of the Red Army put an end to this new crime of the Nazis."[59]

Perhaps the Soviets hoped that the introduction of this evidence would claim some of the media attention that was focused on the sensational objects introduced by American prosecutors, the shrunken head and the tattooed skin. The claim that the semi-tanned

Figure 12. The samples of soap alleged to be made from human fat introduced by Soviet prosecutors at Nuremberg.

human skin was evidence that a Nazi research program in tanning human skin had been interrupted only by the victorious advance of the Red Army appears to have been an attempt to replace the Americans with the Soviets as the true deliverers of Europe from this particular manifestation of Nazi barbarity—presaging many other instances of attempted Cold War one-upmanship.

AFTER NUREMBERG: ILSE KOCH

The International Military Tribunal at Nuremberg concluded on October 1, 1946. A series of other trials soon began to take place in the American zone (and also in the other occupation zones and in other countries) including several involving specific concentration camps. On April 11, 1947, the second anniversary of the liberation of Buchenwald, a trial of former Buchenwald officials, guards, and prisoners was begun at Dachau. Defendant Number 15 was Ilse Koch.

Ilse Koch made a sensational entrance at her trial. Though she had been incarcerated continually since her arrest by American authorities on June 30, 1945, she appeared in the courtroom at Dachau visibly pregnant. How exactly she became pregnant has never been explained, though of course reporters and others were quite willing to speculate that she might have at some point been joined in her cell for an illicit liaison by an American guard, or a German national, or a foreign worker. A co-national named Fritz Schaeffer is often implicated, though there is no real proof of his role.[60] A less titillating alternative is that a family member or other visitor might have smuggled a container of semen to her during a visit, which she

Figure 13. Ilse Koch on trial at Dachau, 1947.

then used to impregnate herself. However, she became pregnant, the result was only to intensify the contempt many felt for her, and to contribute still more to the hypersexualized image of her that witnesses and prosecutors would promote. Her pregnancy was widely interpreted as a deliberate attempt to forestall a death sentence.

While the legal and judicial details of the trial are of interest in their own right, they are beyond the scope of this article. It is sufficient to note that (1) The defendants were charged with participating in a "common design" to subject unnamed non-German individuals interned at Buchenwald to "killings, beatings, tortures, starvation, abuses and indignities"[61] (2) That if convicted of participating in the common design, individual defendants would then be sentenced in accordance with the nature of the particular offenses committed by those individuals (3) The judicial deck was

Figure 14. Konrad Morgen testifying on June 10, 1945, at the trial of Buchenwald defendants held at Dachau.

stacked against the defendants: "The tribunals at Dachau did not conform to customary civilian judicial procedures as practiced in the U.S. and Britain, and were in fact, more akin to military courts-martial, even though not all the accused, such as Ilse Koch, were (or had been) military personnel. Hearsay testimony was allowed, witnesses for the prosecution were paid for their time, and affidavits (written testimony) were permitted, which precluded defense attorneys from cross-examining those who had submitted the affidavits. Prior to the start of the Buchenwald tribunal, sworn statements were taken by the prosecution from key witnesses, only a few of whom would testify at the trial. The tribunal was only meant to consider crimes committed after January 1, 1942, when the wartime Allies were constituted as the United Nations. Further, those on trial were referred to as the "accused" and not "defendants", and there was no presumption of innocence."[62]

Witnesses for the prosecution testified that Ilse Koch had reported prisoners to SS guards knowing that they would be beaten, that these punishments instigated by her resulted in severe injury, in at least one case leading to the death of a prisoner, and that she had on at least one occasion beaten a prisoner herself. Witnesses also testified that she had had prisoners killed for their tattoos, which were harvested and fashioned into lamp shades and other objects, such as photo album covers. Konrad Morgen testified at the trial, lending support to the accusations of prisoner abuse against Ilse Koch, but also reporting that his surprise search of the Koch home in the summer of 1943 had revealed no objects made of human skin, and that at that time he had seen no evidence and had heard no rumors about Ilse Koch's involvement in the procurement or use of tattooed human skin. Ilse Koch's defense requested that the human-skin objects Ilse Koch was accused of possessing be produced by the prosecution, but this was never done during the trial. The shrunken head and a large example of preserved human skin with a tattoo was displayed at the trial.

On July 28, 1947, the American periodical *Newsweek* carried an article about Ilse Koch entitled "*Witch of Buchenwald: The Record of a Sadist*" which included photos taken from the Koch family photo albums referred to by the prosecution as having been bound in human skin.[63] All thirty-one defendants in the Buchenwald trial were convicted on August 12, 1947.

Figure 15. It was this page from the July 28, 1945 issue of Newsweek that alerted Ilse Koch to the fact that her personal photo albums were in American possession.

When given the opportunity to make a final statement after her conviction, Ilse Koch pointed out that the presence of the photos in the *Newsweek* article clearly showed that her photo albums were in the possession of American authorities, and that despite requests by the defense, the prosecution had never produced any lampshades or photo albums in court. Had these photo albums been entered into evidence, argued Koch, she could have refuted the charge that her albums were bound in human skin.

Within minutes of the announcements of the sentences, defense lawyers were presented with two photo albums belonging to Ilse Koch. These albums had apparently been in the possession of the prosecution throughout the trial, though their existence had not been disclosed to the defense. Examination of the photo albums revealed that they were not covered in human skin, but in leather or cardboard.[64] Defense attorneys were understandably outraged. This information was included in the petition for review that would be filed subsequent to Ilse Koch's sentencing.

The Buchenwald defendants were sentenced on August 14, 1947.

Ilse Koch received a life sentence. The most sensational charges against her, those involving tattooed human skin, undoubtedly contributed to the lengthy sentence she had received, though no real proof of these charges had ever been presented. Her attorneys submitted a petition for review of her sentence, arguing that the punishment meted out to Ilse Koch was excessive in light of the offenses actually proven against her. A lengthy review by American legal authorities followed, which resulted in a recommendation to reduce Ilse Koch's sentence to four years imprisonment. On June 8, 1948, General Lucius Clay, Military Governor, signed an order reducing Ilse Koch's sentence according to this recommendation. This order was not publicly announced, however, until September 16, 1948.[65] Clay's reduction was justified in part on the grounds that the human-skin charges against Ilse Koch had not been satisfactorily proven at trial.

Figure 16. General Lucius D. Clay, Military Governor. General Clay was savagely criticized for reducing Ilse Koch's prison sentence. Clay was responsible for governing the American zone in Germany during the difficult years of the Berlin Airlift.

What followed was a firestorm of outrage in the American and international media. The rumors about Ilse Koch's alleged murder of prisoners to produce lampshades, purses, gloves, and album covers of their tattooed skins had been (largely uncritically) repeated again and again in films, newspaper and magazine stories, and in stories told by camp survivors, veterans, and others. This barrage of titillating and sensational coverage had an immense impact on public opinion: the few voices of reason that attempted to objectively evaluate the charges and evidence against Ilse Koch were shouted down. It was suggested that Koch's sentence must have been reduced because of political pressure of some sort, that American justice had been somehow subverted.

UNITED STATES SENATE INVESTIGATION

Shortly after the announcement of General Clay's reduction of Ilse Koch's sentence, on September 16, 1948, as newspapers across America decried and mocked the decision, the United States Senate decided to hold hearings into the events surrounding Ilse Koch's trial and its aftermath.[66] Outrage at the hearings centered on the fact that the reviewing authorities had questioned the credibility of some witness testimony in reaching their judgment for reduction, something that the Senators claimed was improper in light of typical civil procedure. The trial itself, of course, was far from anything resembling normal civil procedure, so it is not clear why the review process would be held to such stringent standards.

Figure 17. Senator Homer S. Ferguson of Wisconsin, who chaired the Senate committee investigating Ilse Koch's sentence reduction.

The Senators, giving voice to the public outrage against Ilse Koch that had been whipped up first by American military authorities immediately after Buchenwald's liberation, and then amplified by the steady drumbeat of salacious and often fact-challenged stories in the press, sought desperately to find a way to reinstate Ilse Koch's life sentence. The possibility of having the President order General Clay to reinstate the life sentence was considered, as were other, seemingly more realistic options. The Army was instructed to review the evidence and testimony against Ilse Koch, that which had been presented at Nuremberg, and at the trial of Buchenwald defendants at Dachau in 1947, as well as evidence that might exist that had not been used in any judicial proceeding, and determine whether she could be re-tried by American authorities without incurring accusations of double-jeopardy.

The idea that there might be a mass of unused evidence against Ilse Koch that could be used to secure a new conviction was pushed by William Denson, the chief prosecutor at the Buchenwald trial, in a letter to the editor that was widely published on September 27, 1948. According to Denson:

> "When Ilse Koch was sentenced to life imprisonment on August 14, 1947, I knew that justice had not been too stern with her. If I had been told that in a little more than a year the military government authorities in Germany would commute her sentence to four years, I simply would not have believed it.
>
> I know Frau Ilse Koch well. I was chief prosecutor at her Dachau trial. I know the extent, the quantity, and the quality of the evidence against

this handsome, red-haired, blue-eyed woman. Indeed, there was so much evidence – almost everybody released from Buchenwald had something to say about Ilse Koch's habits – that I was forced to use restraint in presenting my prosecution before the tribunal. I presented only 10 witnesses when there were scores more anxious to testify against her. For the sake of brevity, I deliberately under-emphasized the overwhelming case against her.

I know much more about Ilse Koch than went into the trial proceedings, too. Investigations resulted in a full picture of this incredible woman, much of which could not be brought into the trial. A large part of her story cannot be told here either, because it is so unspeakably indecent.

Suffice it to say that Ilse Koch developed into a sadistic pervert of monumental proportions, unmatched in history." [67]

Contrary to Denson's widely trumpeted claims, Army legal authorities were unable to find a vast body of additional evidence on which to base a new prosecution. On 29 and 30 November, 1948, Army Judge Advocate General personnel in Europe submitted documents to the Civil Affairs Division, Special Staff, at US Army Headquarters.[68] These documents offered an assessment of the pros-and-cons of the available evidence, and included testimony that had been provided in the trial of Hermann Goering at Nuremberg. On December 9, 1948, an interim report, which was never officially finalized, was released by the Senate committee in late December, 1948. The report concluded that:

"In our opinion, the findings and sentence of the trial court were justified by the record. Ilse Koch's guilt having been established by the judgment of the trial court and the confirmation of that judgment by the reviewing authority, there is no persuasive mitigating evidence in the record to justify any reduction in the sentence. Most of the defendants tried with her could avail themselves of the plea that they were part of a military organization and as such were obliged to carry out orders regardless of how much they personally opposed them.

In contrast, every act committed by Ilse Koch as shown by the evidence was that of a volunteer. Such voluntary action, contrary to every decent human instinct, deserves utter contempt and denies mitigation. There is no evidence that any other officer's wife or any other woman participated in the operation of the camp. Being a woman made her participation more unnatural and more deliberate.

The finding of guilty established that Ilse Koch, of her own volition and without provocation, violated the laws of war and the standards of common decency. Four years' imprisonment is not just punishment for her acts." [69]

There is much in this passage that is cringe-worthy. In contrast to the committee's findings, the reviewing authority had found "persuasive mitigating evidence", the prosecution had engaged in clear misconduct, and the defense of "superior orders", which the Senate committee seemed to endorse, had been specifically rejected by the International Military Tribunal and other American war crimes trials. If anything, military members should be more aware of and sensitive to

Figure 18. William D. Denson, (far right) prosecutor at the Dachau trial of the 31 Buchenwald defendants, lobbied strenuously to keep Ilse Koch in prison.

their obligations under the laws of war than civilian personnel. Karl Otto Koch had, after all, been executed by the SS for (in part) having prisoners executed without proper approval. The committee suggested that mitigation could not be considered because Ilse was a civilian and her acts were voluntary, thereby implicitly repudiating the very basis of American war-crimes trials. That Ilse Koch was a woman somehow seemed immensely important to the senators. Why did Ilse Koch's alleged conduct inspire such revulsion and seem to demand such severe punishment?

Nineteen forty-eight was a hard-fought election year, at least until Tuesday, November 2. American legislators did not seem especially interested in entertaining even the possibility that the reduction in Ilse Koch's sentence had been justified, or that some reduction was merited: here was a perfect opportunity to be seen to be on the right side of history and justice. The American public had been tutored by the press that Ilse Koch's case

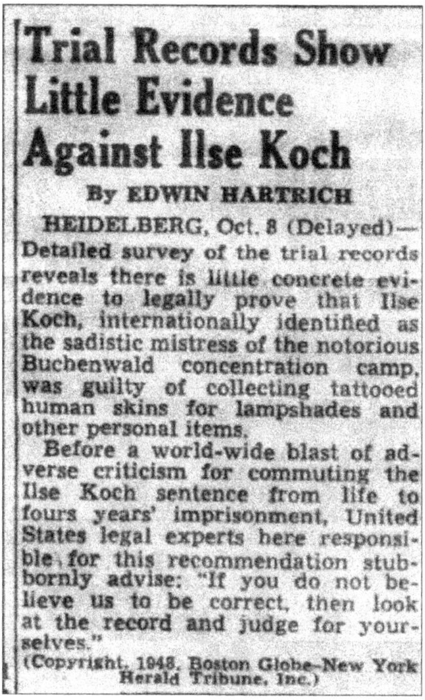

Trial Records Show Little Evidence Against Ilse Koch

By EDWIN HARTRICH

HEIDELBERG, Oct. 8 (Delayed)—Detailed survey of the trial records reveals there is little concrete evidence to legally prove that Ilse Koch, internationally identified as the sadistic mistress of the notorious Buchenwald concentration camp, was guilty of collecting tattooed human skins for lampshades and other personal items.

Before a world-wide blast of adverse criticism for commuting the Ilse Koch sentence from life to fours years' imprisonment, United States legal experts here responsible for this recommendation stubbornly advise: "If you do not believe us to be correct, then look at the record and judge for yourselves."

(Copyright, 1948, Boston Globe-New York Herald Tribune, Inc.)

Figure 19. There were a few reporters who tried to present the case against Ilse Koch objectively, but these voices were largely drowned out by the flood of misinformation appearing in news articles about her.

was black-and-white, and nuance was the last thing on the mind of the senators. The Jewish Telegraphic Agency reported on September 29, 1948, that U.S. Representative Arthur G. Klein of New York "today wired Royall [Kenneth C. Royall, Secretary of the Army] asking him "either to overrule General Lucius Clay's order of June 8, commuting the sentence, or to find a new capital crime for which she [Ilse Koch] could be brought to trial again." [70]

During World War II, Gordon Allport and Robert Knapp organized so-called "rumor clinics" to try to limit the destructive effects of rumor. [71] These were attempts to fact-check rumors in regular newspaper articles. An effort like this happened spontaneously in the fall of 1948, when public hysteria over the reduction of Ilse Koch's sentence was being fanned in Washington, D.C. On October 13, 1948, the first in a series of articles about the case of Ilse Koch appeared in the *New York Herald Tribune*. This article was datelined Heidelberg, October 12, by Edwin C. Hartrich. The title of the article, "The Evidence Against Ilse Koch: No Proof Commandant's Wife Collected Tattooed Human Skin" states Hartrich's conclusion succinctly. While Hartrich got several minor facts wrong in the article, his review nevertheless captured the essential truth that with respect to the human skin allegations, nothing more than circumstantial and hearsay evidence had been produced in Ilse Koch's trial. Four readers' replies were printed in the same newspaper on October 20: all excoriated Hartrich for his challenge to the conventional wisdom. The *Herald Tribune* published another attempt at clarifying matters on October 29: "A Review of the Ilse Koch Case: What the Public Knows About the Woman Charged with Atrocities at Buchenwald", by Walter Millis. After reviewing the available evidence, Millis concluded that "it seems rather difficult not to accept the statement of General Lucius D. Clay, who had final responsibility for review of the case." On November 8, 1948, another review of the case by the Munich correspondent of United Press, Josephine Thompson, entitled "Frau Koch's Case Shows Evidence Was Circumstantial" was published in American newspapers.[72]

But there were many more cries for Ilse Koch's head: On September 28, 1948, an article entitled "Leniency for Sadist" appeared in the Jamestown (NY) Post-Journal; a story in the Philadelphia Inquirer on October 6, 1948, entitled "Former Hospital Head Assails Army's Action on Ilse Koch" added more fuel to the fire. These stories, and many more like them, helped reinforce and sustain the public animus against Ilse Koch.

RUMORS OF INJUSTICE

THE GERMAN TRIAL

The Senate investigation headed by Homer Ferguson was not a legal proceeding that itself could have any direct consequences for Ilse Koch, but it could and did have profound and indirect consequences for her. Despite Denson's widely publicized claims to the contrary, the Army's review of the Ilse Koch case concluded that there was not sufficient evidence that had not already been presented at the Buchenwald trial to justify a new proceeding, and that re-trying her using evidence that had already been presented at the Buchenwald trial would be improper, as this would constitute double-jeopardy.

The Senators who had so savagely criticized General Lucius Clay for following his conscience and reducing Ilse Koch's sentence wanted desperately to find a way to undo his reduction of her sentence. After it became clear that no American legal proceeding would be able to accomplish this goal without significant damage to American prestige, the idea of using German courts to retry Ilse Koch was raised. The 1947 Dachau trial of Ilse Koch had only considered accusations against Ilse Koch having to do with non-Germans. It was a war-crimes tribunal, and nations cannot commit war crimes against their own citizens. Once the occupation of Germany came to an end, however, German court systems would come into existence with the power to try German citizens for offenses committed against other Germans. The Senators knew that Ilse Koch would be in American custody until October 17, 1949. As it happened, the occupation was ended and Germany was partitioned into the Federal Republic of Germany and the German Democratic Republic before Ilse Koch's release from prison.

At first glance it would seem unlikely that there would be much enthusiasm in a newly-established German state to initiate a war-crimes trial against one of its own citizens. By 1948 the German population had grown tired of denazification, of the constant public reminders of Nazi barbarity, and of German collective guilt. Eugen Kogon, the Buchenwald survivor whose book *Der SS Staat* had been published in 1948, was concerned that "if Hitler returned, many would follow him again."[73] Germans were being asked to support the West in its intensifying conflict with the Soviet Union, which would manifest itself in the Berlin Blockade and the Berlin Airlift from the middle of 1948 until the middle of 1949, while Germany's Nazi past was (it seemed to many of them) continually thrown into their faces.

Konrad Adenauer, first Chancellor of the Federal Republic of Germany (West Germany) pursued a policy of reintegrating war criminals into the fabric of West German society. The Federal Republic was not only not seeking new cases to prosecute, it was acting to release those who had been convicted as soon as possible. Many who had committed and been convicted and sentenced for far greater crimes than Ilse Koch had been released by the time she was transferred to German custody in October, 1949.

There were, however, many potential winners and only a few potential losers (Ilse Koch and her children) in a German trial of Ilse Koch. The new German government stood to gain favor with America. American authorities, painted into a corner by their creation and enthusiastic dissemination of the Ilse Koch-lampshade story, only to find the story challenged by their own Military Governor, hoped a new German trial would show the world that the American propaganda about Ilse Koch wasn't propaganda, after all, and the charges against her were credible.

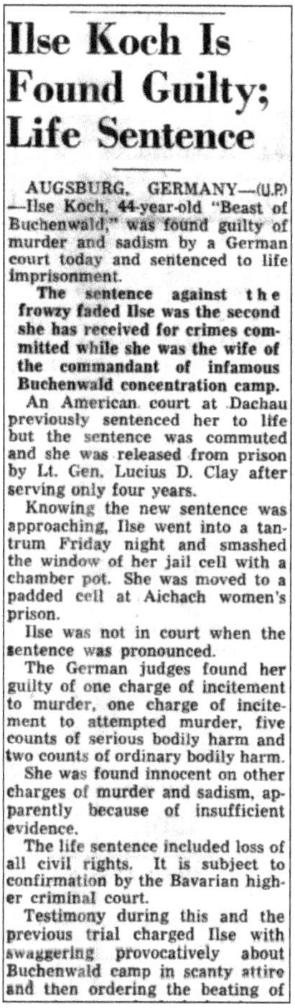

The German government also stood to gain credibility as genuinely anti-Nazi. The Soviets and their (as of October 7, 1949) East German puppets claimed the mantle as the true anti-Fascist, anti-Nazi German spirit, painting West Germany as the original source of Nazism and as reluctant to hold Nazis to account. Germans themselves were tired of being blamed for Nazi atrocities. The decline in war crimes prosecutions and the policy of reintegration might be easier to defend if a very visible prosecution took place. Trying Ilse Koch would deflect attention away from ordinary Germans squarely onto the Nazi elites, a convenient displacement of blame onto a small group no one was eager to defend. Uniformly despised, Ilse Koch was an appealing target for West German prosecution.

Ilse Koch's last trial began in Augsburg on November 27, 1950. She was formally charged

> **Ilse Koch Is Found Guilty; Life Sentence**
>
> AUGSBURG, GERMANY—(U.P.)—Ilse Koch, 44-year-old "Beast of Buchenwald," was found guilty of murder and sadism by a German court today and sentenced to life imprisonment.
>
> The sentence against the frowzy faded Ilse was the second she has received for crimes committed while she was the wife of the commandant of infamous Buchenwald concentration camp.
>
> An American court at Dachau previously sentenced her to life but the sentence was commuted and she was released from prison by Lt. Gen. Lucius D. Clay after serving only four years.
>
> Knowing the new sentence was approaching, Ilse went into a tantrum Friday night and smashed the window of her jail cell with a chamber pot. She was moved to a padded cell at Aichach women's prison.
>
> Ilse was not in court when the sentence was pronounced.
>
> The German judges found her guilty of one charge of incitement to murder, one charge of incitement to attempted murder, five counts of serious bodily harm and two counts of ordinary bodily harm.
>
> She was found innocent on other charges of murder and sadism, apparently because of insufficient evidence.
>
> The life sentence included loss of all civil rights. It is subject to confirmation by the Bavarian higher criminal court.
>
> Testimony during this and the previous trial charged Ilse with swaggering provocatively about Buchenwald camp in scanty attire and then ordering the beating of

Figure 20. *The Dispatch,* Moline, IL, January 15, 1951.

with committing acts of abuse against German internees at Buchenwald, charges that were similar to those that had been made against her at the 1947 Dachau trial. The charges at Augsburg referred only to Germans: this vacated any possible objections to her prosecution on the grounds of double jeopardy. For the first time, she was also formally and specifically charged with offenses related to the procurement and use of tattooed human skin. In late December, 1950, Ilse Koch suffered a mental breakdown of some sort, and was removed from the courtroom for mental evaluation.

The last trial of Ilse Koch was reported in American media as a triumph of justice. Dr. Kurt Sitte, a German scientist who had testified at the 1947 Dachau trial against Ilse Koch, was at the time a professor at a college in New York. Sitte's accusations against Ilse Koch were rehearsed again in public. Court proceedings came to a close on January 11, 1951.[74] The verdict of the court was announced January 15, 1951. The court found that there was insufficient evidence to sustain the charges against Ilse Koch related to tattooed human skin. Ilse Koch was found guilty of one count each of incitement to murder and incitement to attempted murder, five counts of incitement to severe physical maltreatment of prisoners, and two counts of physical maltreatment.[75] She was again sentenced to life in prison. Her appeal was heard and denied on April 23, 1952. Ilse Koch committed suicide by hanging on September 2, 1967.

When Ilse Koch committed suicide, very few Nazi war criminals tried by the Allies were still in custody. Albert Speer had been released after serving his 20-year sentence the year before, and Rudolf Hess would serve another twenty years of his life sentence as the sole prisoner in Spandau, dying in 1987. Amnesties and a variety of other programs and policies had already led to the release of virtually all Germans convicted of war crimes in Allied war crimes tribunals by late 1958. Speer and Hess were war criminals of an entirely different caliber than Ilse Koch, who never had any official position in the Nazi regime. Why was Ilse Koch still in jail in 1967? Arthur Smith put it best:

> "Ironically, Ilse would undoubtedly have been released with the others, [meaning other war criminals tried by the Allies] had Clay not changed her sentence and thus prompted Ferguson's intervention, which ultimately led to the German trial."[76]

It was General Lucius Clay's insistence on following his conscience in reducing her sentence that unintentionally condemned Ilse Koch to die in prison. Had Clay not reduced her sentence, Ilse Koch would most likely have been released with the others convicted in military tribunals in the 1950's. But Clay's reduction of her sentence set in motion a series of events that would ensure that she would never be freed: her four-year sentence kept her in American custody long enough for Senator Ferguson and his colleagues to hold their hearings, and to instigate the process that recruited the new Federal Republic of Germany to the effort to achieve the "justice" for which the news media and public clamored.

An interesting point of comparison in this regard is the case of Erika Flocken. Flocken was a physician who was assigned to the "Muhldorf

Figure 21. Mühldorfer Hart Concentration Camp Memorial, http://www.kz-gedenk-mdf. de/m%C3%BChldorf-prozess.

Ring", a series of Organisation Todt labor camps associated with Dachau. In her capacity as chief physician she selected prisoners too weak to work to be transported to Auschwitz, where they would be murdered in the gas chambers. She was also convicted of withholding needed medical supplies from prisoners, causing much needless suffering and death: approximately 4,000 prisoners died at Muhldorf during her tenure. Erika Flocken was romantically involved with the Muhldorf camp commandant, Walter Langleist, who was himself convicted of war crimes and hanged by the Allies. Erika Flocken was convicted at her Dachau trial and sentenced to death. Her sentence was commuted to life imprisonment, reportedly in part because American authorities did not want to execute a woman, and she was released from prison in 1957.[77] Had Ilse Koch's sentence not been reduced, her fate would probably have been very similar to Erika Flocken's.

Was Ilse Koch's life sentence just? The course of justice was very uneven in and across the many war crimes trials that were conducted in Europe after WWII. Some Nazis convicted of crimes like those of which Ilse Koch was convicted also received harsh sentences, especially those tried soon after the war. Others convicted of similar and sometimes much worse crimes were given considerably lighter sentences. Many others escaped justice completely. If we focus not on the sentence but on the actual time served, however, Ilse Koch's treatment comes into clearer focus as a definite outlier: she served far more time than many war criminals convicted of far more serious offenses, such as *Einzatzgruppen* commanders.[78]

AFTER NUREMBERG:
THE OUTCOME FOR RUDOLPH SPANNER

The rumors about Rudolf Spanner and his alleged soap factory were well-known and extensively publicized in Poland, though these rumors do not appear to have captured the attention of the world, and America, as did the rumors about Ilse Koch. The following quotation may be found today on the website of a prominent Holocaust genealogy organization:

> "One of the worst crimes committed by the Nazies [sic] has been in Stutthof. Professor Rudolf Spanner, an SS officer and 'scientist', was owner of a small soap factory located in Danzig. In 1940, he invented a process to produce soap from human fat. This 'product' was called R.J.S.?'Reines Judische [sic] Fett'? which means 'Pure Jewish Fat'. Hundreds of inmates were executed for the 'production' of soap. Rudolf Spanner was very proud of his invention. Following testimonies of some survivors, he used to spend hours and hours to admire his 'invention'. At the liberation, the Allies discovered chambers full of corpses used for the production of soap. After the war, Rudolf Spanner was not arrested and continued his 'researches'..."[79]

This quotation conflates the soap produced at the Danzig Anatomic Institute with the rumors about soap manufactured from the bodies of Jews that had circulated since late 1942 in Poland. That Rudolph Spanner had Jews from the Stutthof concentration camp transported to the Danzig Anatomic Institute for the (small-scale) commercial production of soap from their body fat was broadly accepted in Poland from the time of the liberation in the spring of 1945 until quite recently. Within weeks of the introduction at Nuremberg by American prosecutors of a shrunken head and some pieces of tattooed human skin allegedly procured by Ilse Koch, Russian prosecutors introduced pieces of soap from the Danzig Anatomic Institute and pieces of tanned human skin allegedly produced by Rudolph Spanner. We have seen what became of Ilse Koch. What happened to Rudolph Spanner?

Rudolph Spanner had left Poland in early 1945 and returned to Germany, where he, like Ilse Koch, made no attempt to hide his identity, living openly in Hamburg, attempting to resume his professional life. He appears to have had three contacts with authorities. He was denounced to police in 1947 by residents of his apartment building after they saw reports from the Nuremberg trials discussing the Soviet introduction of the soap from the Danzig Anatomic Institute. He was arrested by the British in May 1947 (Hamburg was in the British zone of occupation) and released after three days of interrogation. Spanner admitted that during the process of removing flesh from cadavers in order to obtain bones for anatomic models used to train medical students, a soapy substance was incidentally produced. He used this material in the production of his anatomic models to make the joints work smoothly. Spanner denied using human bodies to produce soap for commercial purposes. Spanner was released without charges.[80]

He was investigated by police (the Flensburg Public Prosecutor) again in November 1947, when he was "accused of war crimes by Max Knott, who read the description of the "soap factory" in George Rehberg's book *Hitler und die NSDAP in Wort und Tat*" (1946)." Spanner again explained his use of the soapy material for the production of anatomic models, and was again released without charges.[81] His last contact with authorities occurred in late 1948, when he went through a denazification process in which he was cleared of any suspicion of having participated in war crimes.[82]

Rudolph Spanner became a professor at the Institute of Anatomy at the University of Cologne, and in 1957 became Director of the Institute. Spanner died of a heart attack on August 31, 1960. Even though the accusations of committing war crimes in the production of soap from human fat against Rudolph Spanner were as widely accepted in Poland as the claims that Ilse Koch killed prisoners for their skin to be used in the manufacture of household objects were in Europe and the United States, no attempt was ever made to extradite Spanner from Germany to bring him to Poland for trial. Arguably, what happened to Rudolph Spanner is very much like what ought to have happened to Ilse Koch. Why was Ilse Koch's postwar life so different?

THE POWER OF RUMOR

Whether one believes that there were ever human-skin lampshades, and if so, whether Ilse Koch had anything to do with them, is immaterial to the demonstration of the awesome power of rumor that emerges from this story. Ilse Koch's defense attorneys in the 1947 Dachau trial knew what they were up against:

> "The power of propaganda and mass suggestion can hardly be better illustrated than in the case of Ilse Koch. Long before the trial she was publicly known as the 'Witch of Buchenwald'—condemned as a green-eyed,[83] red-haired, nymphomaniac who enjoyed collecting lampshades and other objects of human skin. Stories were eagerly spread from person to person, the press embellished them with sensational details; each new report added unlikely details to the picture."[84]

The Ilse Koch story is a two-part story. The first part of the story involves the original rumors associating Ilse Koch with objects made from tattooed human skin. This association occurred sometime before the liberation of Buchenwald on April 11, 1945. The second part of the story began on

April 16, 1945, the day the citizens of Weimar were marched past the table at Buchenwald on which rested pathological specimens, preserved tattooed human skin, shrunken heads, and a lampshade said to have been made of human skin.

ORIGINS

There are at least two possible origins of the original rumors associating Ilse Koch with lampshades and other objects made of human skin. One possibility is that Ilse Koch did, in fact, select prisoners with appealing tattoos, have them murdered, and then make or cause household objects, including lampshades and photo albums, to be made from their skin. Of this there has never been any convincing evidence: certainly there has never been any physical evidence. Ilse Koch was accused of possessing photo albums covered in human skin, but these were found to have been made from leather and cardboard, not human skin. The lampshade displayed on the table at Buchenwald did not have any decorations that might have been tattoos, and the object itself disappeared. Despite all this, proving a negative is not easy. We cannot be sure that there were not such objects, and if there were, whether Ilse Koch had any role in their procurement or production.

The other possibility is that Ilse Koch had no connection to any objects made from human skin, and that the rumors making this connection arose through the mechanisms outlined by various theorists of rumor, such as

Allport and Postman, Rosnow, and Shibutani. While we cannot say with absolute certainty at this remove that this is how the rumors originated, we can observe that all the ingredients necessary for the formation of such rumors were present at Buchenwald, in spades. These include uncertainty, potentially relevant and important events, and the existence of a constellation of facts (the existence of a tannery, a bookbindery, a research program involving tattooed human skin, Ilse Koch's arrest by the SS in 1943) that could easily be integrated into a coherent and compelling narrative involving Ilse Koch, her equestrian activities, her sexual predilections, her cruelty toward prisoners, and these other facts.

FROM RUMOR TO WORLDWIDE INFAMY

American authorities displayed the tattooed skin materials at Buchenwald to show the world how barbarically the Nazis had treated prisoners. They soon had a propaganda tiger by the tail, however, and the public's insatiable demand for more information about the objects was obligingly met by journalists who were happy to uncritically repeat and embellish the rumors about Ilse Koch, especially as Ilse Koch, the sometimes green-eyed, sometimes blue-eyed, always red-haired, nymphomaniac Nazi, was a figure guaranteed to be highly interesting to the reading and watching public.

The American director Billy Wilder made a short film about Buchenwald, which included a shot of the display table and narration connecting the lampshade to the wife of the Commandant, who was soon identified as Ilse Koch. Newspapers ran stories mentioning Ilse Koch and tattooed human skin throughout the summer of 1945, but the story really gained worldwide notoriety when it was brought up at the International Military Tribunal at Nuremberg in late 1945. The lampshade and shrunken heads were apparently too good a prop for the Allied prosecutors to pass up, though there really wasn't much background available to explain their significance: Andreas Pfaffenberger's affidavit was a useful justification for their display, however. So the shrunken head and lampshade were introduced at Nuremberg.

Ilse Koch, by any historical measure an utterly insignificant figure, was now mentioned in the same breath as the twenty-one highest-ranking Nazi war criminals the Allies had decided to put on trial before the world. This turn of events catapulted Ilse Koch into the international spotlight. While the rumors surrounding Ilse Koch were somewhat inchoate at the time of the liberation, they were refined as time passed by the processes of leveling and sharpening and assimilation, and many of the stories told about her by survivors began to contain some common elements and themes. These common elements and themes may have been shaped to some degree by the questioning of investigators and prosecutors. So much of the testimony about Ilse Koch was hearsay, prosecutors were eager to show conclusively that objects made from human skin were in her possession, and that her role in a chain of events that began with the selection of a tattoo on a living person, followed by the murder of that person, and finally, a piece of tattooed skin with a tattoo identified to that same person appearing on an object in her possession could be validated.

As the rumors about Ilse Koch became widely known, and as the investigatory net was cast more widely leading up to the 1947 Dachau trials, more and more survivors came forward with stories about Ilse Koch. This was also true as the German trial was prepared: Ilse Koch was arrested by the Germans on October 17, 1949, but did not go on trial until December, 1950. As time passed and the Ilse Koch case was given wide publicity, more and more people, including survivors, came into contact with stories about her. Survivor's memories are subject to the same mechanisms of potential distortion and confusion that plague all of us.[85]

One such mechanism that can play havoc with memories of historical events is called the imagination inflation effect.[86] This occurs when we come to believe that events (or actions) we have only imagined are things that we actually experienced, or did. As survivors heard or read stories about Ilse Koch's behavior, they might very well have visualized the details as they heard them, perhaps relating and conflating them with other events in their memories—perhaps inserting themselves into similar scenes. Later, the Ilse Koch stories might seem like things that were part of their own autobiographical memories.

Another mechanism that can affect our recollections of long-ago events is a process called misattribution.[87] This occurs when information that has entered our consciousness through one means, such as having been seen in a film, or experienced as a dream, or seen as a home movie of our childhood, is adopted by us as an actual memory. In such cases we misattribute something we have seen or heard to our own experience. A common example of this in Holocaust studies are claims made by survivors of having experienced certain iconic movie scenes, such as Dr. Mengele performing selections on the ramp at Auschwitz, even though the timing of theirs and Mengele's tenure at Auschwitz may not have overlapped at all.

The fact that in many cases there may have been a delay between hearing rumors or "camp lore" about Ilse Koch's alleged tattooed skin obsession while still imprisoned at Buchenwald, and the lurid and sensational news reports that began to appear with some frequency first during the Nuremberg tribunal, then during the 1947 trial, and then again after Clay's sentence reduction in late 1948, yet again upon her transfer to German custody in late 1949, and finally on the occasion of her final sentencing in January, 1951 created many opportunities for imagination inflation and source misattribution to occur as survivors read or heard these reports, reflected on them, discussed them with others. The highly emotional tone of the rumors and reports complicates this picture still further: the prospect of holding to account a person accused of such heinous crimes may very well have compromised the integrity of some memories that were only vague or suggestive.

Decades later, these processes were still at work, and new accusations have been made against Ilse Koch as recently as 2014. Jack Werber, a survivor of Buchenwald who wrote a memoir entitled *Saving Children: Diary of a Buchenwald Survivor and Rescuer*[88] related a story about Ilse Koch and tattooed human skin. In his telling, Ilse Koch would sit astride a white horse by the camp gate each morning and note the prisoner numbers of prisoners with appealing tattoos. Werber claimed that he worked alongside a German prisoner named Hans who had tattoos of a boat and the German phrase "Ich liebe dich" (I love you), and that Ilse Koch noted his prisoner number. Werber dated this event to the initial building of the Gustloff Werke buildings, which would have been relatively early in the camp's history.

Werber reported that "Hans" was murdered and his skin harvested for his tattoos. So far, this story is structurally similar to many of the early survivor tattoo testimonies. In Ilse Koch's 1947 and 1950 trials prosecutors struggled to directly connect her to tattooed skin that could be unambiguously traced to a known prisoner, whose fate could be tied to her intervention. The most detailed testimony along these lines came from a prisoner named Kurt Froboess, who described a tattoo of a sailboat on a prisoner named Jean, that he later saw on Ilse Koch's photo album.[89] Werber says that one of Hans' tattoos was a boat.

Werber seemingly provides the missing link that prosecutors sought in vain during the trials of Ilse Koch: he states that he saw these very distinctive tattoos, that he identified unequivocally as belonging to Hans, on a lampshade in Ilse Koch's villa at Buchenwald when he was sent there to perform repairs after it was damaged in the American bombing raid of August 24, 1944.[90] If this testimony were believable, it would actually exonerate Ilse Koch, because she had been in custody in Weimar for more than a year, and according to Konrad Morgen, the entire contents of her home, which definitively did not contain a human-skin lampshade with tattoos, had been shipped to Czechoslovakia a year before Werber supposedly saw the lampshade in the Koch home.

Werber's 2014 memoir is interesting in that he also remembered other atrocious conduct by Buchenwald guards that have not, to my knowledge, been corroborated by other survivors. For example, he claimed that prisoners were fed food containing ground glass, and given poisoned coffee. He remembered the camp clock being stopped at 3:15 to memorialize the exact time of liberation, when in fact photographs of the clock taken for months after the liberation show that it was still keeping time. He also claimed that Buchenwald prisoners were given soap made from the fat of Jews murdered by the Nazis.[91]

THE "KOMMANDEUSE": A CONVENIENT TARGET?

The fact that Ilse Koch was a woman clearly played a role in her treatment by the press and by the courts. It was not so much what she did, but that she was a "she" that mattered: that fact somehow made her alleged crimes "unnatural and more deliberate", according to the Senators. Alexandra Przymbel discusses the gendered interpretations of perpetrator behavior that doubtless contributed to public attitudes about Ilse Koch, and were in no small part responsible for her fate.[92] News stories about Ilse Koch frequently focused on her sexuality, and journalists seem to have been obsessed with her sexuality and physical appearance.

The article in *Newsweek* which alerted Ilse Koch to the fact that her photo albums must be in the possession of American authorities downplayed the allegations against her involving tattooed human skin and emphasized instead her sexuality and alleged promiscuity:

> "Ilse took the stand on July 10 to deny that as wife of the Buchenwald commander, Karl Koch, she collected shrunken heads or lampshades made of human skin. But there is evidence that Ilse did beat prisoners, and expose them to cruel and unusual punishments out of pique, whim, or sadistic enjoyment."[93]

And a few lines later:

> "Ilse was a nymphomaniac. From 1930 on, some of the best people to play around with were Nazis and SS men. Her marriage to Koch was no love marriage, but a good and steady entrée to SS-circles. Koch knew that she was never faithful to him, but for that matter he wasn't faithful to her either. At Buchenwald evidence introduced at the trial reveals that she would ride her prize stallion down to the camp to view the incoming prisoners. Although the fact that she was looking for "tattoos" for lampshades made the headlines, more often she was looking for a prospective lover. Those who struck her fancy were assigned to her house as servants"[94]

Her physical appearance was always of special interest to journalists, some of whom were apparently quite taken with her:

> "She is still attractive, despite her rather blowzy brown sack suit, her short socks, bare legs and saddle shoes. Flaming titan hair, emerald-green eyes, and a schoolgirlish complexion belie the fact that she is 40. On prison diet she has reduced 40 pounds, until her figure, despite a too-prominent derriere and a still-conspicuous bust, is almost boyish." [95]

Others found her to be much less attractive. Edwin C. Hartrich, who undertook to evaluate the evidence brought against Ilse Koch in the Dachau trial and concluded that there was no proof she had collected tattooed human skin described her as ". . . a short, dumpy straw-blonde German woman, with a putty-like complexion."[96]

Still others found her distressingly unremarkable. Anticipating Hannah Arendt's popularization of the phrase "banality of evil" after Adolph Eichmann's 1961 trial in Jerusalem, a Newsweek article observed that:

> "The really terrifying thought that creeps into one at all these war-crimes trials is that the defendants always look astoundingly normal. There is no art to read the mind's construction in the face. Ilse Koch doesn't look much different from the little German waitress who is waiting on tables one block away at the swank American Officers' mess—but who has her job today because she was an inmate here at Dachau."[97]

Ilse Koch was clearly different things to different people: a canvas on which to explore their own sometimes fantastic assumptions and beliefs, but one thing she had surely become in the months after the liberation of Buchenwald was a symbol. The presence of the lampshade on the Buchenwald display table, her alleged association with it, and the titillating sexual stories told about this otherwise unremarkable woman would conspire to create an enduring and widespread image of her as an imaginably cruel, inhumane, sadistic pervert.

Freudian explanations of the Nazi mind were quite common and popular from the time the Nazis came to power in 1933. The American government commissioned several studies of Hitler's psychology, and these were generally couched in distinctly psychoanalytic terms. Hitler's relationships with his parents were seen as contributing to his authoritarianism; his obsessive anti-Semitism was attributed to his possible Jewish ancestry; his relationship with his niece, Geli Raubal (who took her own life in 1931) was suspected of featuring bizarre sexual perversions; his thirst for power, some thought, might have resulted from his reputed monorchidism. This tendency to apply psychoanalytic categories extended beyond Hitler, and indeed was recruited to explain the "German" mind itself.

Much of this seems a bit silly in retrospect, the more so as the "authoritarian personality,"[98] a concept directly derived from Freudian thinking which survived the war as a possible psychological explanation of what had happened, fell on hard times as empirical studies failed to confirm the basic assumptions of the approach (the concept survives today as "right-wing authoritarianism").[99] One wonders why those who had been so eager to apply psychoanalytic thinking to understanding the motivations of Nazis failed to see any Freudian overtones in the dogged persecution of Ilse Koch. The obsession with her sex, her looks, her wearing of provocative clothing, her promiscuity and sexuality, her domineering nature, her power over men, evidenced by their ubiquity in news stories about her suggests that these aspects of the story were of central importance to readers. Perhaps some of those men who worked so hard to condemn Ilse Koch were exhibiting signs of reaction formation: because they were titillated by the stories about her, excited by the stories of prisoners brought into her bed, by her co-opting of the masculine symbol of the horse, by their secret wish to be dominated and sexually used by her or someone like her, they had to scream their revulsion and disgust from every rooftop, relentlessly pursuing her to hide their attraction to her.

TESTIMONY

Another factor in Ilse Koch's fate was the existence of so many former prisoners of Buchenwald willing to testify against her. Rudolph Spanner worked in a small, closed environment in which he came into contact with relatively few outside the small circle of workers and assistants who helped run the small facility he led. Ilse Koch was known directly to some probably small number of Buchenwald inmates, and indirectly to many more through the stories told about her. Prisoners "heard" that Ilse Koch had behaved in ways that supported the charges against her, and passed what they had heard from one to another. These stories were repeated at her various trials, and the fact that so many survivors told the same stories was interpreted as evidence that these stories were based in fact. Hearsay may be converted into something more convincing when it becomes a false memory: when people come to believe that they were involved in events about which they had only heard, hearsay can come to masquerade as eyewitness testimony.

Generally speaking, hearsay evidence is not admissible in American courts, though there are many exceptions to this prohibition. When hearsay evidence is admitted, rules of evidence often permit challenging the credibility of the person presenting the hearsay evidence as a defense against such evidence. Challenging the credibility of witnesses who had been the victims of such monstrous treatment may not have been easy in war crimes tribunals, especially when the alternative may have been accepting the credibility of accused (not alleged) war criminals.

In retrospect, the evidence initially produced against Rudolf Spanner was at least as damning as any that was ever produced in support of the allegations against Ilse Koch. There was actual soap produced from human fat found at the Danzig Anatomic Institute, and Rudolph Spanner admitted that he had been responsible for the manufacture of this soap, which was reportedly used in cleaning facilities at the Institute.[100] The rumor that the Nazis produced soap from the bodies of Jews appeared earlier and was more widespread than the rumors about Ilse Koch and tattooed human skin. There are, in fact, striking parallels between the two cases in everything except the ultimate outcome. In both cases there was a "core of truth" that served as a substrate upon which rumors could plausibly be built.

OTHER CRIMES

Further differentiating the cases of Ilse Koch and Rudolph Spanner is the fact that Ilse Koch actually did commit crimes, whereas Rudolph Spanner apparently did not. Ilse Koch was convicted of incitement that led to the injury of some prisoners and to the death of some prisoners. This had two consequences. First, judgments against her were prejudiced as she was identified as a criminal. Why believe the denials regarding human skin of someone who had also denied abusing prisoners, but was convicted nevertheless? Second, it created the opportunity for legal authorities to pass sentence on her. That sentence ought to have been based solely on those crimes of which she had been convicted, and of which there was credible evidence. But the fact that sentence would be passed created the opportunity for the authorities to smuggle into that sentencing process their own beliefs about Ilse Koch, and human skin tattoos, and lampshades, and perhaps impose a sentence that would punish her for what they believed about her rather than what had been proven. And it seems that that is exactly what did happen.

Ilse Koch died in prison, while Rudolph Spanner spent only a few days in custody and then lived the rest of his life in freedom. I began this paper with the idea that understanding rumors, their creation and evolution, was an important part of understanding the different courses the lives and deaths of Ilse Koch and Rudolph Spanner took. It seems clear now that the social and psychological mechanisms that led to the development of rumors about these two individuals operated similarly in their respective cases. The publicity given the rumors about Ilse Koch was more widespread than was the publicity given the rumors about Rudolph Spanner: Ilse Koch was a villain in the eyes of the world, and especially in the United States, whereas the rumors about Rudolph Spanner were confined mainly to Poland. But in both cases, rumors that appear to have formed spontaneously as plausible hypotheses to explain complicated fact-patterns were adopted by authorities and publicized to serve social or political purposes.

Ilse Koch's fate was not worse than Rudolph Spanner's because the rumors about her were any more plausible, or believable, or morally reprehensible. Ilse Koch's fate was worse because she happened to be in the American zone of occupation at war's end. The propaganda juggernaut that began on the display table at Buchenwald on April 16, 1945, drove American authorities to continue to pursue legal action against her to satisfy the public's thirst for vengeance against their creation, the "Beast/Bitch/Witch of Buchenwald". Rudolph Spanner's good fortune was that he was, at war's end, out of reach of those who might have persecuted him: the Poles or Russians. The British and later the Germans were not hounded by an incessant drumbeat of media pressure to bring Rudolph Spanner to "justice", as the Americans were in the case of Ilse Koch. As a result, their investigations could occur in a less superheated atmosphere, and perhaps permit the cold light of reason to operate in place of the hysteria and emotion that surrounded the case of Ilse Koch. Had Rudolph

Spanner found himself in Poland in February, 1946, when the Russian prosecutor introduced the testimony and physical evidence against him at Nuremberg, his future might have looked more like Ilse Koch's.

THE LAMPSHADE

Lawrence Douglas' fascinating article entitled "*The Shrunken Head of Buchenwald: Icons of Atrocity at Nuremberg*"[101] discusses the symbolic importance of the objects introduced at the IMT: the shrunken head and tattooed skin from Buchenwald introduced by American prosecutors, and the pieces of soap from the Danzig Anatomic Institute introduced by Soviet prosecutors (Douglas does not mention the tanned human skin also introduced by the Russians). Douglas' insightful analysis identifies the shrunken head, and the tattooed skin, as representing the atavistic dimension of Nazi barbarism. These objects can be seen as evidence of the Nazi attack on civilization itself: as a rejection of the normative standards embodied in modern civilized life, and as an endorsement of pre-civilized behaviors that incite revulsion and disgust in the modern civilized mind.

The soap, on the other hand, represents something terrifyingly modern: the industrial commodification and exploitation of humans for their constituent parts. Douglas provides a penetrating analysis of these two different interpretations of these objects in light of the moral and legal frameworks of the IMT itself. Douglas also points out that the soap allegedly produced from humans was widely discussed in Freudian terms: excrement, and therefore cleanliness, and therefore soap, play significant roles in psychoanalytic thinking. The irony of producing soap from the bodies of people forced to live in filthy and squalid conditions in the camps is extreme.

Douglas is appropriately skeptical about the particular evidentiary value of these objects: the shrunken head is, as we now say, what it is, but neither it nor the tattooed skin was never convincingly connected to lampshades or to Ilse Koch, and if there was soap made from human fat, it apparently was not done so as part of any industrial or semi-industrial enterprise. What is interesting is that while most of these objects disappeared at some point, the one that continues to capture the public imagination is the lampshade putatively associated with Ilse Koch. The soap-making myth has been debunked relatively effectively: the objective reader searching the internet today should come away with the view that the Nazis did not engage in the production of soap from fat harvested from the bodies of Jews. The shrunken head has disappeared, but it was never tied to any individual, and its significance did not really extend beyond the symbolic significance articulated by Douglas.

But the lampshade stubbornly persists in Holocaust mythology. A 1956 issue of *Male* magazine included a story predictably titled, "The Bitch of Buchenwald".[102] (Other offerings in the same issue included, "The Back Street Doll", and "The Fish That Ate My Indian".) The expose (as it was

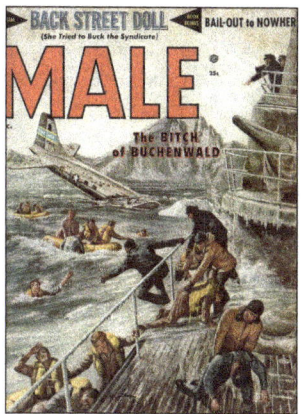 

Figure 22. Illustration from the article about Ilse Koch in a 1965 issue of Male magazine.

labelled) on Ilse Koch was authored by Charles V. Nemo. The quite lengthy story is written in a faux-academic and objective tone, and clearly reflects significant effort. The story gets many facts right, and features quotes from Eugen Kogon, Konrad Morgen, and Kurt Titz. But the story also includes elements fabricated by Mr. Nemo or someone else to spice up the story: converting Kurt Titz into a kind of sex slave, for example, and describing Ilse Koch's predilection for staking inmates to a post and shooting various body parts off them before delivering the coup de grace with a (clearly drawn) P.08 Luger pistol. This skillful blend of fact and outrageous fiction could easily present an air of credibility to the uncritical reader, a species in no shorter supply in 1956 than is the case today.

In 1975 a film entitled "Ilsa: She-Wolf of the SS" was produced in Canada. The film is part pornography and part horror, but it nominally plays on the Ilse Koch story. Ilse Koch spelled her name with an "e", not an "a", but the reference to her is unmistakable when one sees on the film's publicity poster the lines, "My name is ILSA! I turned my lovers into

Figure 23. "Ilsa, she wolf of the SS".

Lampshades!" The film was actually shot on the set that had been used for the American television series *Hogan's Heroes*: an interesting connection, as Robert Clary, who played Corporal Louis LeBeau on *Hogan's Heroes,* was a real-life survivor of Buchenwald. Just a few years ago the journalist Mark Jacobson embarked on a quest to validate the authenticity of a lampshade that came to light in New Orleans after Hurricane Katrina as the human skin lampshade from Buchenwald.[103] An initial DNA test seemed to confirm that the lampshade was made of human skin, but subsequent testing supported the conclusion that the material was cowhide. The lampshade still provokes our interest.

Was there a lampshade made of tattooed human skin? Dr. Harry Stein, Curator of the *Buchenwald Gedenkstaette,* authored a response to a "Frequently Asked Question" on the website of the *Buchenwald Gedenkstaette* entitled "Is it true that the SS made lampshades of human skin in the Konzentrazionslager Buchenwald?"[104] Stein argues that there were three lampshades that might have been made of human skin. Two Buchenwald survivors, Gustav Wegerer and Joseph Ackermann, testified in the 1950 German trial of Ilse Koch that they had personally seen a lampshade made of human skin with tattoos, and that Karl Koch had personally commissioned the manufacture of the item in 1941. Wegerer also claimed that he inferred from a conversation between Karl Koch and an SS physician named Muller that Ilse Koch was personally involved in the selection of the decorative motifs for the lamp. The lamp base was constructed of a human foot and shinbone, according to these witnesses. Stein credits this testimony, and refers to this first lampshade as the "real" one.

According to these witnesses, the lamp was delivered in August 1941 to the Koch villa on the occasion of Karl Koch's birthday. Shortly after this public debut, SS leadership became aware of the lamp and confiscated it. It is worth noting that the 1950 trial in which these witnesses testified was the only one that specifically addressed the lampshade charges against Ilse Koch, and reached the conclusion that these charges could not be proven. Furthermore, if this lampshade had been confiscated by the SS leadership, one wonders why Konrad Morgen had not heard about it, as he was the SS judge assigned to investigate the Kochs.

Wegerer had made several contributions to *The Buchenwald Report,* compiled in the first few weeks after the liberation, and did mention human skin objects:

> "Beginning in fall 1940 SS Captain Muller worked in the pathology department. He was then called to the Obersalzberg [Berchtesgaden]. On orders from Berlin, Muller initiated the project of peeling off the tattooed skin from the bodies of dead or murdered prisoners, tanning it and producing lampshades out of it. How many lampshades were produced from human

skin I can no longer say precisely today. But on many occasions several hundred pieces of tattooed human skin, tattooed in various manners, were sent to SS Colonel Lolling, the chief of Section D III of the Main Economic and Administrative Office of the SS in Oranienburg."[105]

This report was compiled in April 1945. At that time, Wegerer attributed the impetus for the human-skin lampshades not to the Kochs, but to "orders from Berlin" transmitted through SS Captain Muller. It was not until five years later, after all the intervening publicity about the Kochs and the lampshades, that his memory included the visit from Karl Koch and the conversation about Ilse Koch and her selection of the decorative tattoo motifs.

The second lampshade discussed by Stein is the one pictured on the exhibit table at Buchenwald on April 16, 1945. Stein points out that it disappeared shortly after being exhibited on the 16th, and was never seen again. More on that in a moment.

There was also a third lampshade alleged to be made of human skin that was exhibited as such during the years when the Memorial was an institution under the control of the East German government. First exhibited in 1954, this was a smaller lampshade, perhaps for a night-table. When Germany was reunified and the management of the Memorial began to change, this lampshade was tested and found to be not of human origin. Of the three candidates for the human-skin lampshades potentially connected to Ilse Koch, one (the first) was supposedly confiscated by the SS and presumably destroyed. The third was tested (long after Ilse Koch's suicide) and found not to be made of human skin. The remaining candidate, the lampshade exhibited on the table at Buchenwald on April 16, 1945, is thus the only possibility that may remain to determine whether there were lampshades made of human skin. This lampshade was probably the one in Pister's office, which Morgen said Pister had described to him (per Koch) as made of human skin.

WHAT HAPPENED TO THE SECOND LAMPSHADE?

The lampshade story can live on because the object that was exhibited on the table at Buchenwald as a human-skin lampshade is lost to history. No modern scientific analysis or technique can ever lay to rest the question of whether the lampshade was made of human skin, because the object has disappeared. What happened to it? What became of this object, so famous the world over? The answer is unexpectedly undramatic: it (or at least most of it) was brought home to Indiana by an American soldier. It was later sold to a collector who has never been identified, who then supposedly disposed of it as too ghastly to possess.

The soldier was Major Lorenz C. Schmuhl. Major Schmuhl was Deputy Warden of the Indiana State Prison, located in Michigan City, Indiana. Lorenz served briefly as the first American commander of the newly liberated Buchenwald. The camp was liberated late in the day of April 11, 1945. Schmuhl arrived at the camp late on the 15th and left the camp on the morning of April 25, when he was reassigned to a Displaced

Persons camp at Wiesbaden.[106] During his tenure at Buchenwald Schmuhl and his staff began the process of obtaining much-needed resources for the camp, organizing the prisoners in conjunction with the International Camp Committee (composed of long-serving inmates), and generally trying to bring order and support to the camp.

Schmuhl's diary entry for Monday, April 16, 1945, describes the visit of many American soldiers to view the camp, and also the visit of approximately 1,000 German civilians from nearby Weimar. It was on this occasion that a table exhibiting gruesome artifacts was on display, and widely photographed. The table contained anatomical specimens, two shrunken heads, pieces of what was reported to be tanned human skin with tattoos, and the lampshade said to be made of human skin. While this was only Schmuhl's first full day at Buchenwald, he had apparently already heard the rumors about human skin being made into household objects, as he mentions them in his diary entry for the day:

> "Sights to [sic] horrible to mention. Lamp shades, book covers etc made from Human skin. When a man came into Camp that was tattooed and the guards or Officers, Officers wives wanted the skin, the man would be killed that night. One of the officers wives had handbags, uppers of her slippers, and gloves made from human skin. Wonder what kind of people would do these things, surely not human beings."[107]

Schmuhl's initial report did not associate the lampshade with the officer's wife who reportedly had these human skin objects, and did not identify the officer's wife as Ilse Koch, but this connection was made just a few days later in an article by Sigrid Schultz of the *Chicago Tribune*:

> "Maj. L.C. Schmuhl, formerly of the staff of the Indiana State prison at Michigan City, Ind., had pieces of what seemed to be parchment on his desk. One was decorated with a nude woman, another a blackish picture of napoleon and his eagle. The parchment was human skin. Whenever a prisoner reached camp and the jailers found he was tattooed, the wife of the former camp commander, SS Leader Karl Koch, was asked if the design appealed to her. If it did, the man was taken to the hospital and given a lethal shot. Then the skin was tanned and presented to Frau Koch, who made pocketbooks and lampshades out of it. A lamp in the possession of the American Army is made of human skin and bones."[108]

Figure 24. The three different panel types present in the Signal Corps Photo of the lampshade are highlighted here.

Schmuhl left Buchenwald on April 24, and took with him at least three of the pieces of tattooed skin that had appeared on the exhibition table that the world saw on April 16, and at least eight panels from the lamp-

Figure 25. In these photos I have outlined the lampshade panels laying on Schmuhl's table in the same colors seen in the above photos of the lampshade.

shade that was displayed on the table. The lampshade was composed of eighteen panels: six arrowhead-shaped pieces that made up the top of the lampshade, and 12 alternating side panels: six narrow, and six wide panels. One top panel, one wide side panel, and one narrow side panel appear to have been missing when the photograph was taken. At least three of the arrowhead-shaped top panels, three large side-panels, and

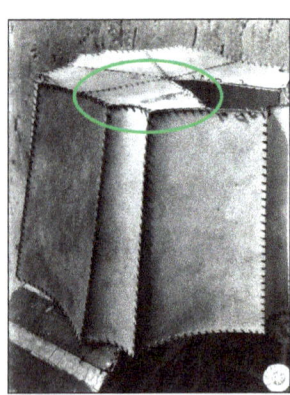

Figure 26. The Signal Corps photo with the area of discoloration on one top panel highlighted.

at least two narrow side panels were taken by Schmuhl. The *Indianapolis Star* published an article[109] about Major Schmuhl on February 27, 1949, a few months after the news of Ilse Koch's sentence reduction and the subsequent blitz of publicity about her had erupted and Senate hearings convened. A photograph accompanying the article (entitled "Buchenwald Horror Still Haunts Sleep of Hoosier Warden") shows a wicker table with the three examples of preserved tattooed skin, and several clearly recognizable panels of the lampshade from the exhibit table at Buchenwald. The caption of the photo reads, "These skin souvenirs are grim reminders to L.C. Schmuhl, deputy warden of Indiana State Prison at Michigan City, of his work at the infamous Nazi prison camp at Buchenwald soon after it was liberated in 1945."[110]

We know that Schmuhl brought his (at least) eight pieces of the lampshade back to Indiana, and that three pieces were already missing when the Signal Corps photo was taken. What became of those three missing pieces, or of the seven pieces of the lampshade (two arrowhead-shaped top pieces, two large side panels, and three small side-panels) that remain when we subtract the eight known to have been taken by Schmuhl is unknown. We know that Schmuhl brought at least these pieces of the lampshade back to Indiana through photographic evidence provided by Schmuhl himself. We can trace the pieces of the lampshade through three photographic sources: the lampshade as it appears on the table exhibited at Buchenwald on April 16, 1945, the Signal Corps photo, and photographs of Schmuhl with the artifacts in his home in Michigan City, Indiana, published in the *Indianapolis Star* in 1949. We can be reasonably sure that the three photographic sources are all presenting the same object because of two features of the lampshade: the fact that three of the 18 panels of the lamp were missing when the lampshade was exhibited on April 16, 1944, and a unique pattern of discoloration on one of the arrowhead-shaped panels from the top of the lamp. One of the arrow-head shaped top pieces has a distinctive dark discoloration parallel to one of the outside edges that is visible in both the Signal Corps photo and the photos of the pieces in

Schmuhl's home. This is the panel immediately to the left of the missing panel in the Signal Corps photo. Photos of the exhibit table containing the lamp are taken from ground level, so this piece is not visible in photos or films of the lamp from that day. The geometry, number, and shape of the panels visible on the lampshade on the table do correspond to the lampshade in the Signal Corps photo. Still photos taken on the day of the exhibit, such as the one above with prisoners holding a sheet behind the artifacts, do not show either the missing panels or the area of discoloration on the one top panel. There is, however, a film that was made on April 16, 1945, that does show the lampshade from several angles. The angle, distance, and resolution of the shot make it impossible to say whether any of the top pieces has the distinctive pattern of discoloration, but it does appear that the lampshade on the table in the film is missing one of the arrowhead-shaped top pieces,[111] as is the lampshade in the Signal Corps photo. While we cannot be 100% certain, given the quality of the film, we can be reasonably sure that the lampshade on the table missing one of the top pieces in the film is the one in the Signal Corps photo, which

Figure 27. The arrowhead-shaped lampshade panel in the green circle appears to be the one circled in green on the Signal Corps photo of the more-or-less intact lampshade above.

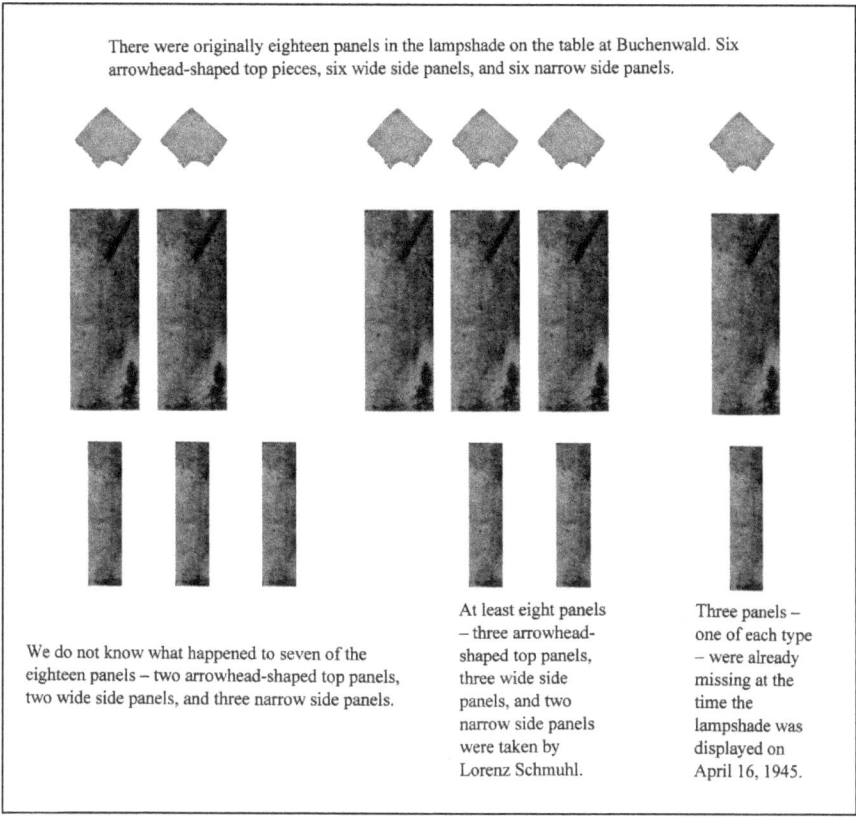

Figure 28. This summarizes our knowledge of the whereabouts of the eighteen panels of which the lampshade displayed on the table at Buchenwald was originally comprised.

provides much more detail and reveals the area of discoloration on one of the arrowhead-shaped top pieces. Whether this area of discoloration was a tattoo or not is unknown and not readily discernible from the photos, but it does offer a means of identifying the panel.

In October, 1948, the whereabouts of the lampshade became a matter of urgent concern and intense publicity. When the Senate opened an investigation into the matter of Ilse Koch's sentence reduction, which was announced in September, 1948, Senators wanted to use the alleged human-skin lampshade as evidence against Ilse Koch. An article datelined Munich, Germany and published in many American newspapers on October 6 and 7, 1948, with headlines such as "Tattooed-Skin Lamp Shades Said 'Missing'",[112] "Tattooed Skin Lampshades Tagged as Evidence in Ilse Koch Case Disappear",[113] and "Army Says Souvenir Hunters Have Evidence Against Koch".[114] Of course, no tattooed skin lampshades had ever been "tagged as evidence." Indeed, no lampshades had ever been "tagged as evidence."

There was a widespread but false impression that the human-skin lampshades had been introduced as evidence at Nuremberg. A few pieces of tattooed human skin were introduced as evidence, and these were linked to Ilse Koch and to lampshades by the hearsay testimony of Andreas Pfaffenberger. An article datelined Nuremberg, December 13, 1945, carried the headline, "Human Head, Lamp Shade of Skin are Shown as Evidence",[115] though neither the lampshade that had been exhibited on the table at Buchenwald nor any recognizable pieces of it (none of which appear to have had any tattoos on them) were introduced at Nuremberg. Three years later, many assumed that the lampshade had been introduced at Nuremberg: "the tattooed-skin lampshades in the Ilse Koch case are lost, American war crimes officials here said today ... The skin and other gruesome ornaments from the Buchenwald concentration camp possibly repose among the souvenirs in the home of some American, they said ... Prior to the Buchenwald trial, the skin and other articles were sent to Nuernberg for use in the Nuernberg trial of Hermann Goering and other

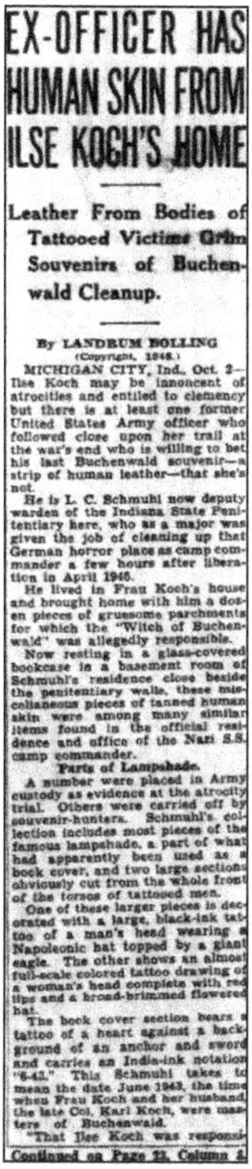

EX-OFFICER HAS HUMAN SKIN FROM ILSE KOCH'S HOME

Leather From Bodies of Tattooed Victims Grim Souvenirs of Buchenwald Cleanup.

By LANDRUM BOLLING
(Copyright, 1948.)

MICHIGAN CITY, Ind., Oct. 2—Ilse Koch may be innocent of atrocities and entiled to clemency but there is at least one former United States Army officer who followed close upon her trail at the war's end who is willing to bet his last Buchenwald souvenir—a strip of human leather—that she's not.

He is L. C. Schmuhl now deputy warden of the Indiana State Penitentiary here, who as a major was given the job of cleaning up that German horror place as camp commander a few hours after liberation in April 1945.

He lived in Frau Koch's house and brought home with him a dozen pieces of gruesome parchments for which the "Witch of Buchenwald" was allegedly responsible.

Now resting in a glass-covered bookcase in a basement room of Schmuhl's residence close beside the penitentiary walls, these miscellaneous pieces of tanned human skin were among many similar items found in the official residence and office of the Nazi S.S. camp commander.

Parts of Lampshade.

A number were placed in Army custody as evidence at the atrocity trial. Others were carried off by souvenir-hunters. Schmuhl's collection includes most pieces of the famous lampshade, a part of what had apparently been used as a book cover, and two large sections obviously cut from the whole front of the torsos of tattooed men.

One of these larger pieces is decorated with a large, black-ink tattoo of a man's head wearing a Napoleonic hat topped by a giant eagle. The other shows an almost full-scale colored tattoo drawing of a woman's head complete with red lips and a broad-brimmed flowered hat.

The book cover section bears a tattoo of a heart against a background of an anchor and sword and carries an India-ink notation "6-43." This Schmuhl takes to mean the date June 1943, the time when Frau Koch and her husband, the late Col. Karl Koch, were masters of Buchenwald.

"That Ilse Koch was responsi-

Continued on Page 23, Column 1.

Figure 29. This article, which explicitly mentions Schmuhl's possession of pieces of the Buchenwald lampshade, was published just a few days before Schmuhl denied having any pieces of the lampshade.

top Nazis . . ." "The articles never came back to us,' a war crimes spokesman said."[116]

Some versions of this October 6/7, 1948 article reporting the loss of the lampshade also contain versions of the following statement:

"L.C. Schmuhl, deputy warden at the Indiana state prison, said Wednesday he had two pieces of tattooed skin, but none of the lampshades reported missing in the Ilse Koch case. Schmuhl gave this version of how the skins came into his possession: He was serving as major [sic] in the AMG (American Military Government and was attached to the Third army [sic] at the time General Patton's Third army [sic] liberated Buchenwald. As General Patton's army pushed forward, Schmuhl was assigned temporarily as commanding officer at Buchenwald for about two weeks until relieved by an officer from the First army [sic]. A war crimes investigating team moved in during his brief term as commander and removed evidence from the camp, including the lampshades made of human skin. Schmuhl said the team left behind the two pieces of skin which he brought home as souvenirs."[117]

This was, we know, a false statement. In fact, a completely contradictory account had appeared in an article published a few days earlier in the October 3, 1948 issue of the *St. Louis Post-Dispatch*, under the headline "Ex-Officer Has Skin From Ilse Koch's Home", which included the following statement:

> "Now resting in a glass-covered bookcase in a basement room of Schmuhl's residence close beside the penitentiary walls, these miscellaneous pieces of tanned human skin were among many similar items found in the official residence and office of the Nazi S.S. camp commander ... Schmuhl's collec-

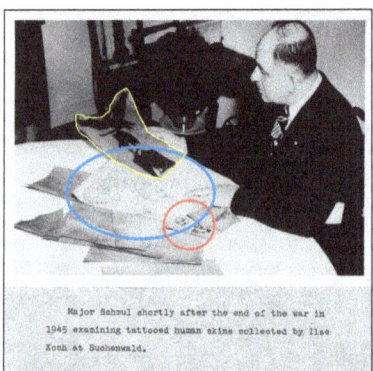
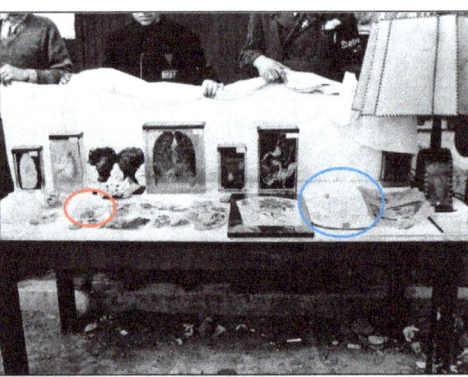

Figure 30. This photo shows three pieces of tattooed skin on Schmuhl's table. The "lady in the hat" (blue circle) and "heart/arrow" (red circle) were on the table at Buchenwald. The Napoleon/eagle piece was not on the table at Buchenwald, but the French-captioned photograph appears to show Schmuhl in uniform holding this distinctive piece of tattooed skin.

tion includes most pieces of the famous lampshade…"[118]

No photos accompanied this article, though the author (Landrum Bolling) did provide detailed descriptions of some of the items shown in photos of Schmuhl's souvenir collection that would appear in later articles. On January 4, 1949, just a few months after Schmuhl had denied having anything more than two pieces of tattooed skin from Buchenwald, William Denson, who prosecuted Ilse Koch at Dachau, published an article in Look magazine entitled, "Why should Ilse Koch go free?" This article was accompanied by several photographs, including one captioned, "Squares of tanned human skin, photographed recently, were brought to America by Lorenz C. Schmuhl. An American AMG major attached in Buchenwald in 1945, he says skins came from Ilse's home."[119] The photograph clearly shows three pieces of tattooed human skin, and the several pieces of the lampshade from the exhibit table at Buchenwald, considerably more than the "two pieces of tattooed skin" to which Schmuhl had publicly admitted.

A few weeks later, on February 27, 1949, Schmuhl himself was featured in an article in the *Indianapolis Star*. This article was accompanied by the same photograph that had appeared in the Look article a few weeks earlier. The article contains the following misleading statement: "He [Schmuhl] lived, at the time, in the Buchenwald commander's big, lavish house—and there found the evidence of Ilse Koch's inhuman hobby."[120] The Koch house had been damaged in the American bombing raid of September 24, 1944, and Ilse Koch's possessions had been removed a year before that (1943) by the SS in any case on the occasion of the Koch's arrest. Schmuhl frequently repeated the falsehood that he had acquired the skin souvenirs from Ilse Koch's house, reinforcing the putative connection between Ilse Koch and the pieces of tattooed skin. The lampshade and shrunken head were apparently in the office used by Hermann Pister, which Schmuhl took over.

THE CHESS SET

The lampshade pieces and examples of human skin with tattoos were not the only souvenirs Schmuhl brought home from Buchenwald. In April of 1978 another article[121] recounting Schmuhl's experiences at Buchenwald appeared, this time in the Michigan City, Indiana *News-Dispatch*. This article was accompanied by a photograph that appears to have been taken on the same occasion as the photo that had appeared in the earlier *Look* article, but is from a different angle which shows two hand-carved chess pieces. These chess pieces were part of a set that had been carved by prisoner artisans at Buchenwald and was in the commandant's office when the camp was liberated. Schmuhl took this 32-piece set with him when he left Buchenwald and mailed it home before leaving Europe.

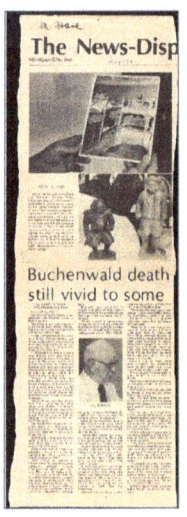

Figure 31. This article in the Michigan City, Indiana News Dispatch on April 4, 1978 showed examples of the chess pieces from Buchenwald.

The descendants of Lorenz Schmuhl returned the chess set to Buchenwald in August, 2002. Unfortunately, this was not the case for the lampshade and other pieces Schmuhl had

Figure 32. "Art in the face of horror". A report in the Weimar Allgemeine on the return of the Buchenwald chess set.

taken: in the 1978 *News-Dispatch* article (which is, by the way, rife with inaccuracies) Schmuhl is quoted as saying, "I never saw the lampshades, but the skin was found by us. It was in sheets bearing large tattoos. The skin was later sold to a collector, but he has since gotten rid of it. He found he couldn't stand looking at it."[122] All that can be said, then, of the whereabouts of the only conclusively identified pieces of the lampshade from the Buchenwald exhibit table, is that they were taken by Schmuhl, retained for some period in Michigan City, Indiana, and then lost to history.

WHY DIDN'T SCHMUHL ADMIT HE HAD THE LAMPSHADE?

Given the significance accorded the lampshades in shaping world opinion about Ilse Koch, we must wonder why Lorenz Schmuhl failed to make the nearly half of the lampshade from the Buchenwald exhibit table in his possession available to the relevant judicial authorities. The lampshades were made an issue at the IMT in December 1945 through Pfaffenberger's testimony, though no lampshades or parts of lampshades were entered into evidence—only some examples of irregularly shaped human skin with tattoos. Schmuhl followed developments related to Buchenwald and to Ilse Koch closely: many of the newspaper clippings used in writing this article came from Schmuhl's papers, which were donated to the United States Holocaust Memorial Museum. Had Schmuhl offered the pieces of the lampshade to the IMT, at least an assessment as to their actual composition might have been made.

Thirty-one people from Buchenwald, including Ilse Koch, were tried at Dachau in the late spring and early summer of 1947. Schmuhl doubtless followed these developments closely: still more witnesses alleging Ilse Koch's role in murdering inmates for their tattoos and making lampshades of their skin came forward. Again, no lampshades or parts of lampshades were entered into evidence, only irregularly shaped fragments of tattooed skin. Again, Schmuhl failed to make available to authorities the parts of the lampshade from the Buchenwald exhibit table in his possession.

When Ilse Koch's sentence reduction from life to four years was announced in September 1948, Senate investigators wanted to examine the lampshades as evidence against Ilse Koch justifying the most severe penalty against her. The fact that the lampshade(s) could not be found was widely publicized. Yet again, Schmuhl failed to make available to the Senators the evidence in his possession that they were actively seeking. This was more than a passive failure to act: Schmuhl was consulted about the whereabouts of the lampshade, and apparently actively lied to investigators seeking information about the lampshades. He reported that he had only two pieces of tanned skin, when he actually had at least three such objects, as well as at least eight pieces of the lampshade from the exhibit table, a thirty-two piece-chess set from the Commandant's office at Buchenwald, a photo album, and likely other souvenirs from Buchenwald as well. Somewhat bizarrely, though, his denial of any knowledge of the whereabouts of the lampshade came only three days after the *St. Louis Post-Dispatch* article confirming his possession of the lampshade panels appeared in print.

Photographic evidence of this was first published for all the world to see in January, 1949, in the *Look* article by William Denson, and again in February, 1949, in the article about Schmuhl in the *Indianapolis Star*. The photographs accompanying these two articles clearly contradicted Schmuhl's earlier claim that he had only two pieces of tanned skin, and clearly showed the panels from the lampshade on the Buchenwald exhibit table.

Why would Schmuhl not make this evidence available to the IMT, or to the judicial authorities at the Dachau tribunal, or to the Senate investigators? He himself would surely have known that they were material to the case against Ilse Koch so publicly discussed during the IMT and during and after the Dachau tribunal. The Senate investigators, and most of the world, labored under the misapprehension that the lampshades had been lost after they had been introduced at the IMT, as many news reports falsely claimed that lampshades had been entered into evidence there. Actually, the lampshade (at least 8/15 of it) had been "lost" almost immediately after it had appeared on the exhibit table at Buchenwald: lost into Lorenz Schmuhl's suitcase or duffel bag on April 24, when Lorenz Schmuhl left Buchenwald for Wiesbaden.

Lorenz Schmuhl died in 1988, so we can only speculate as to possible motives for his actions with respect to the lampshade panels. The most obvious potential motive is embarrassment at having taken them, or fear of criticism for having done so. The difficulty with this possibility is that Schmuhl clearly seems to have relished the publicity his role as the first American commander of the liberated Buchenwald brought him: he gave interviews and was the subject of several newspaper articles, including one in 1949 and another in 1978. We know that he possessed pieces of tattooed skin, panels from the lampshade, a photo album, and the chess set. The photograph accompanying the two 1949 articles show only the tattooed skin and the lampshade panels, though the captions do not identify the lampshade panels as such. Two of the chess pieces appear in the photograph accompanying the 1978 article, which, based on Schmuhl's very distinctive necktie, was probably taken on the same occasion as the photo from the 1949 article.

Another possibility is that Schmuhl might have withheld the lampshade panels until judicial proceedings against Ilse Koch were exhausted out of fear that their appearance might redound to the benefit of Ilse Koch. General Lucius Clay expressed his opinion that the lampshade was actually made of goatskin, which if determined to be true might have had exculpatory benefit for Ilse Koch, though this would not explain Schmuhl's withholding of the lampshade panels before 1948. Perhaps a more obvious reason to withhold them was that none of the lampshade panels included the one thing all the accusers of Ilse Koch agreed they should include if the lampshade was one produced by or for Ilse Koch of human skin: tattoos. This should have been apparent to anyone who had seen the lampshade (or images of it) on the exhibit table at Buchenwald: the panels are all plain, blank, devoid of any decoration. Even if this lampshade had been found to have been made of human skin, something the world will now most likely never know (thanks in part to Lorenz Schmuhl) the absence of any tattoos would make it useless in pursuing the case against Ilse Koch, which was fundamentally rooted in the claim that she rode about Buchenwald looking for men with tattoos that appealed to her. Perhaps worse (in Schmuhl's mind) it might even have helped her case. When we recall that the prosecutors in the Dachau trial had Ilse Koch's photo albums in their possession during the trial but did not provide them to the defense or even admit having them, and then suddenly gave them to the defense within hours of Ilse Koch's sentencing, this potential rationale does not seem far-fetched.

That the appearance of one newspaper article on October 3, 1948, describing Lorenz Schmuhl's collection of pieces of the lampshade from Buchenwald should be followed three days later by numerous articles reporting his denial that he had any of the pieces of the lampshade should excite no interest from Senate investigators, reporters, or others at the

Figure 32. This may be the photo Ken Kipperman saw of a lampshade in the Koch villa at Buchenwald.

time is quite baffling to the modern mind. How could he have gotten away with this? Perhaps the explanation for this lies in the comparatively primitive state of mass communication at that time. Television was in its infancy, though by the mid-fifties a substantial proportion of American homes would have television sets. Radio was a medium that reached a national audience, but much communication was still local. This is one reason that Gordon Allport and others worked so hard to combat rumors: it was difficult to know what people were thinking or being told, and to get accurate information to them, because media markets were so fragmented.

It does seem, though, that if something like the internet had existed in 1948, someone might have noticed Bolling's article on October 3, and also noticed Schmuhl's denials on October 6. The photos that appeared in January and February 1949 might also have been examined and the connection made between the objects in the photos and the lampshade made. As it happened, this connection would not be made for decades, until Ken Kipperman's diligence and ingenuity uncovered it.[123] Kipperman also saw a photo of a room in the Koch villa at Buchenwald with a lampshade that he concluded was made of human skin and contained tattoos. I'm not sure exactly which photo Kipperman was referring to. The above photo was apparently from a Koch family photo album, and may be the photo Kipperman saw. It does not appear to me to exhibit tattoos—the decoration around the bottom appears to be a repeating pattern.

BEAST OF BUCHENWALD?

What should we take away from this long and disappointing tale about Ilse Koch and Rudolf Spanner? Sadly, nothing especially encouraging. Anyone laboring under the delusions that the American system of justice cannot be subverted and used as an instrument of persecution, or that American journalism (then or now) is more concerned about facts than about a good story, or that gender and men's fantasies about women don't affect justice (and business, and education, and . . .) ought to find him- or herself disabused of such quaint notions by this time.

Ilse Koch was no heroine, no martyr for any cause. There can be no posthumous redemption for her. She embraced the worst of Nazism and lived amidst the horrors it created, raising her children as thousands suffered and died a few hundred yards away. But is she the real "Beast" of Buchenwald? It is worth putting her time at Buchenwald in perspective. If we use the nominal figures for admissions and deaths at Buchenwald given in the Buchenwald Report (these figures are known to underestimate the real death totals) and consider that Karl Otto Koch was relieved as Commandant at the beginning of 1942, and that Ilse Koch was arrested in the middle of 1943, never to return to Buchenwald, the below table illustrates the numbers and percentages of admissions to Buchenwald and deaths in the camp during three time periods: when Ilse Koch was the Commandant's wife, when Ilse Koch lived at Buchenwald with her family and Hermann Pister ran the camp, and after Ilse Koch had left Buchenwald.

Years	Admissions	Deaths
1937-1942	41,002 (17%)	5348
1942-1943	35,196 (15%)	4606*
1943-1945	162,782 (68%)	23,508**

The above table summarizes figures for admissions to Buchenwald and deaths in the hospital at Buchenwald for three time periods: when Karl Otto Koch was Commandant of Buchenwald, when Ilse lived at Buchenwald with her children after Karl Otto Koch's departure, and after Ilse Koch was arrested and left Buchenwald permanently.

*Approximately 8,000 Russian prisoners were executed in 1941/2 at Buchenwald. These were not included in the statistics provided in *The Buchenwald Report*.

**Approximately 13,000 prisoners died in late 1944 and early 1945 when they were sent on "death marches" as Soviet and American forces came closer to the camp. These deaths are also excluded from these figures.

Inspection of these figures reveals that eighty-three percent of those admitted to Buchenwald as prisoners could have had no experience with Ilse Koch when her husband was Commandant, the period during which we might expect her influence in the camp to have been greatest. Ilse Koch bore three children between June 1938 and December 1940, so she was pregnant a considerable part of the time that she lived at Buchenwald with her husband. Sixty-eight percent could have had no experience with her at all: they were admitted to the camp after she had been arrested in mid-1943, and could only have encountered her through hearsay. The number of prisoners at the camp and the death rate were both fairly stable during the time Ilse Koch was at Buchenwald. It was after her arrest that large numbers of prisoners began to flood the camp, and conditions began to deteriorate so dramatically. The death rate was higher in 1944-1945 than it had been in the earlier years of the camps existence.

Buchenwald, and the horrors it represents, are tightly bound in the popular mind with Ilse Koch and Karl Otto Koch. Flint Whitlock's volume about them is entitled, "The Beasts of Buchenwald", and it is Ilse Koch whose name is almost never mentioned without her various nicknames (The Witch of Buchenwald, The Red Witch of Buchenwald, The Bitch of Buchenwald) being quickly added. It would be improper to ask whether this identification of Ilse Koch with the horrors of Buchenwald is "fair". Ilse Koch willingly associated herself with the most racist and murderous elements of a racist and murderous regime, benefitted personally from the misery imposed on others, and committed and abetted acts of violence against others.

It is, however, proper to ask whether it is accurate to personify the evils of Buchenwald in the Kochs, especially Ilse Koch. By identifying Buchenwald with Ilse Koch, we attract attention to the sensational but unproven allegations against her, and our attention is deflected away from atrocities that were committed there by others, and by the systemic evils inherent in the Nazi regime and the SS camp system. Eugen Kogon's masterful work showed how widely and deeply the German state and people were involved in the camp system. Hermann Pister, Karl Otto Koch's successor as Commandant, was responsible for the cold-blooded execution of more than 8,000 Russian POWs; prisoners were exploited for their labor by SS-owned enterprises like the DAW[124] and DEST,[125] but also by commercial firms such as the Gustloff Werke[126] and Zeiss[127] in nearby Jena. The Kochs misappropriated funds intended for the camp, and in so doing, worsened the already desperate plight of many prisoners. But the death rate in the camp did not decrease when Karl Otto Koch was replaced as Commandant by Hermann Pister, or after Ilse Koch was arrested in 1943. In fact, it got worse after the Kochs were gone.

A PERFECTLY DISPOSABLE PERSON

In retrospect, it seems clear that including the lampshade on the exhibit table at Buchenwald on April 16, 1945, initiated a chain of events that could not have been foreseen at the time. Those who put it there had been told it was made of human skin, and had heard rumors that Ilse

Koch had murdered prisoners to obtain their tattoos for lampshades. The lampshade had been in the office of Hermann Pister, not in Ilse Koch's home, as so may later stories would wrongly claim. That the lampshade included no tattoos did not, inexplicably, deter the authorities from placing the lampshade on the table and connecting it to Ilse Koch based on the rumors they had heard.

The lampshade and its putative connection to Ilse Koch created a desire to know more about her, and there were many quite willing to provide salacious and titillating stories about her promiscuity and unconventional sex life. These stories raised the temperature still further. Pfaffenberger's testimony at Nuremberg connected lampshades with tattoos to Ilse Koch, and even though no such items were introduced into evidence at Nuremberg, sloppy reporting by journalists ensured that the public thought so. The incessant repetition of the alleged connection between Ilse Koch and tattoo lampshades, though completely unproven in reality, was completely proven in the mind of the public. William D. Denson's attitude is representative:

"What about the notorious human-skin-for-lampshades story? Some claim this story isn't true, since the actual lampshades disappeared in the course of mop-up operations in Germany and were never introduced in evidence at the trial. We feel Ilse Koch is unquestionably guilty whether the lampshade testimony is included or not.

But keep in mind that witnesses testified they saw Ilse pick out prisoners with fancy tattooing; the prisoners disappeared; and later reappeared as lampshades in her living room. Other witnesses testified that Ilse started a fad in lamp shade collecting. It's a proved fact that they had a skin-tannery at Buchenwald."

Of course, the "mop-up operations" into which the lampshade disappeared was actually Lorenz Schmuhl's suitcase, and that was the only "actual" lampshade that was alleged to be connected to Ilse Koch. Other tattoo lampshades are often mentioned—Denson suggests Ilse Koch started a tattoo-lampshade collecting fad, but no examples, or photographs of examples of this burgeoning genre have ever been produced, as far as I know. Denson's fair-mindedness is best gauged by the fact that he withheld the photo albums in the possession of the prosecution from the defense until after the trial. Denson mentions the tannery at Buchenwald as if this confirms his sinister suspicions, but as far as I know no one has ever suggested that human skin was tanned there. The prisoners who worked there were known, but none were called to testify. But none of these details mattered, or matter, for that matter: the lampshade on the table soon became a world-wide symbol of Nazi depravity, and survivor after survivor placed it squarely in Ilse Koch's living room, with or without tattoos.

Having introduced the Ilse-Koch lampshade story to the world, and having fanned the flames of the firestorm of publicity it ignited at Nuremberg, American authorities could hardly hold a trial of Buchenwald defendants without indicting Ilse Koch. And so they did. And given the horrific nature of the testimony against her, the tribunal could hardly give her a mild sentence without thereby invalidating the months of outrage that had already resulted from the government's publicity campaign against Ilse Koch. And so they didn't.

When Ilse Koch's life sentence was reduced in 1948, there was a hopeful moment (if one hopes for justice) of sober analysis and soul-searching. Clay's decision was summarily rejected by many, since everyone just knew that Ilse Koch was guilty. But there were those willing to examine the evidence, to clear their minds of the rumors and stories, examine the evidence and form a judgement, de novo as it were, about the case against Ilse Koch. This tentative voice of reason was soon drowned out in a wave of overheated rhetoric from the US Congress, already inflamed by a contentious national election.

But it was a German court, not an American one, that sealed Ilse Koch's fate. Ilse Koch's trial in Augsburg took place against the backdrop of an ever-warming Cold War, and in an era in which the German people were busy reducing the sentences of war criminals, releasing them, and reintegrating them into German society. Why, then, was she dealt with so harshly? The German court said out loud what Denson's tribunal and the US Senate would not admit: there was no real evidence to substantiate the allegations that had made Ilse Koch famous. Was the court, like Denson, judging her on the basis of crimes of which she had not been convicted, or were there other reasons for her seemingly draconian sentence?

I can only speculate, as the records of the German trial lie beyond both my linguistic and legal capabilities. But as a psychologist, I can't help but note that Ilse Koch's harsh treatment was a very convenient

Figure 34. *Orlando Sentinel*, September 3, 1967.

outcome for many people. There was "guilt fatigue" in Germany in the years following World War II, especially as the concept of collective guilt spread blame for the war and for the Holocaust broadly across German society. Most war criminals were officials of the Nazi regime, a regime for which millions of Germans had voted, and which enjoyed the support of millions more after coming to power. Others were members of the military, a revered institution in which many millions of Germans had served during the war. Trials of individuals associated with the government or the military did implicitly indict a broad swath of German society.

But Ilse Koch had no official status of any sort, and she was not a member of the military. Her unofficial status relieved Germans of the obligation of identifying with her in any way, of considering her in any way representative of them. Those who may have supported the Nazi regime could take satisfaction in her punishment because she and her husband had been accused of crimes against the Nazi state, crimes of which she had been acquitted but for which he had been executed. Those who didn't support the regime could take such satisfaction because she was associated with the corrupt, officious Nazi Bonzen that had lorded it over average Germans during the twelve years of Nazi rule. Most of all, they could dissociate themselves from her because the accusations that had been leveled against her placed her outside the sphere of "average Germans". Whether or not one believed the allegations concerning lampshades, the lurid tales of sexual misbehavior, she was convicted in Augsburg of abusing fellow Germans, making her a "bad apple", owed no consideration on the basis of her Germanness. Ilse Koch's treatment scratched at least four itches: it allowed the new German government to counter Soviet propaganda that West Germany was soft on Nazis; it pulled the American government's sentence-reduction chestnuts from the fire; it created a very visible symbol of Nazi depravity who was emphatically not an average German, and it focused the discussion on crimes that were not racial in nature. Ilse Koch may very well have been an anti-Semite who shared the odious values of the Nazi regime, but if she really was obsessed with obtaining tattoos for her personal use, this essentially exempted Jews as objects of her murderous hobby, as Judaism includes a clear taboo against tattoos.

Missing from this paper, and from most discussions of Ilse Koch, is any attempt to engage her as a person. What was she really like? Why did she do the things she did, make the choices that led her to Karl Otto Koch and to Buchenwald? Most of us are content to see her as the monstrous caricature created by the rumors about her: we have no desire to dig deeper. Why not? We often want to try to "get to know" historical figures as people, to better understand the circumstances and experiences that may have shaped their personalities and their actions in historical events. But there seems to be little interest in digging beneath the public surface in the case of Ilse Koch. I think this is partly because humanizing Ilse Koch might expose us to the risk of being misunderstood, perhaps appearing to empathize with her. Explanation easily slides into justification.

There has been at least one attempt to confront Ilse Koch's legacy in a personal way. The German playwright-actress Gilla Cremer produced a play called The Kommandeuse in 1995, a play consisting solely of a monologue from the sole character, Ilse Koch. The play takes place on the day of Ilse Koch's suicide, and includes excerpts from letters written by Cremer in Ilse Koch's voice. While the monologue is Cremer's rather than Ilse Koch's, the play is a courageous and sensitive attempt to confront Ilse Koch as a person.

Ilse Koch's son Uwe, born to Ilse Koch while she was in American custody in 1947, undertook a campaign to rehabilitate his mother's image after her suicide. He approached the New York Times, and a story by David Binder was published in early May of 1971 and carried under various titles by many newspapers. Uwe Koch had appealed to West German courts for clemency two years before her suicide, and renewed his efforts two years after her death. He was unsuccessful on both occasions.

The final resolution of her case cost Ilse Koch her freedom, and then her life. It cost her children their mother. The children of Nazi bigwigs often struggled to find a place in post-war

Figure 35. Shreveport Journal, May 14, 1971.

Germany, and Ilse Koch's were no exception. Ilse Koch's oldest child, Artwin, committed suicide. The tragedies that befell the Koch family are, of course, insignificant when balanced against the human costs of WWII, of the Holocaust, or even the misery, suffering, and death that happened a few hundred yards from the Koch home at Buchenwald. What seems significant to me is that the Koch family tragedies resulted from public pressure on legal systems rooted in hysterical incitement, incitement based on rumors that were spread by sloppy or lazy reporters and thinkers. The American legal and value system came very close to working: General Lucius D. Clay followed his conscience and the facts, and Edwin Hartrich, Walter Millis, and Josephine Thompson courageously tried to inject some reason into the emotional outcry fomented by William Denson, Homer Ferguson, Lorenz Schmuhl, and so many others. But ultimately, the American system failed, and an injustice was done, even if a German court was the instrument of that injustice.

It would be nice to think that all this was made possible (at least in part) by the comparatively primitive state of mass communication capabilities existing seventy-five years ago that has since given way to television the internet, social media, cell phones, and so on, and that such events would be less likely to happen in this day and age. It appears, however, that things have not gotten better in this regard, and may have gotten a lot worse. Mass communication technology can spread rumors faster and wider than was possible when print newspapers and radio were the primary means of disseminating news. At one time there was just "news", but now we hear about fake news, non-fake news identified as fake news by those who don't like it, misinformation, disinformation, lies, and conspiracy theories: these are now the medium of public discourse. Labelling now seems to be as important as interpreting, evaluating, and understanding information in our culture.

The Ilse Koch case is but another example illustrating that there was never a "golden age" before the internet and social media when public discourse was always rational and measured. We began with a definition of rumor that included the idea that one aspect of rumors that distinguishes such propositions from others is that they lack "secure standards of evidence". If there is any real psychological or cognitive difference between the immediate post-war years and the present time with respect to creation and transmission of rumors, it is perhaps that there is now far less agreement on what a secure standard of evidence might look like. Expertise and authority are no longer concentrated in governmental, political, and academic institutions: people now use the internet to choose among a variety of different often competing, sources for their information. On the bright side, while the "rumor clinics" created and run by Gordon Allport in local newspapers are a thing of the past, fact-checking is now a thing, and an important thing, on the internet and elsewhere. Controversial claims are subjected to analysis, assessed for their veracity and explained. Of course, fact-checkers are far from infallible, and their potential benefit hinges on the willingness of people to use them. In this respect, things may not have changed much since the end of WWII.

NOTES

[1] For a fascinating history of the origin and evolution of this quote, see Garson O'Toole, A **Lie Can Travel Halfway Around the World While the Truth Is Putting On Its Shoes,** https://quoteinvestigator.com/2014/07/13/truth/, retrieved January 27, 2021.

[2] Allport, Gordon, and Postman, Leo. *The Psychology of Rumor*. (New York: Russell and Russell, 1965), p. ix. This edition is a reissue of the original 1947 volume published by Henry Holt.

[3] Goldberg, Amos. (2016). Rumor Culture among Warsaw Jews under Nazi Occupation: A World of Catastrophe Reenchanted. *Jewish Social Studies,* 21(3), 91-125. P.98, footnote 38.

[4] Faye, Cathy. (2007). Governing the Grapevine: The Study of Rumor During World War II. *History of Psychology,* 10(1), 1-21.

[5] Allport and Postman, *The Psychology of Rumor*.

[6] Ibid., p. 2.

[7] Ibid., p. 37.

[8] Ibid., p. 2.

[9] Allport and Postman, p.75.

[10] Ibid., p. 75.

[11] Allport and Postman, p. 99.

[12] Rosnow, Ralph. (1980). Psychology of Rumor Reconsidered. *Psychological Bulletin,* 87(3), 578-591.

[13] Shibutani, Tomatsu. *Improvised News: A Sociological Study of Rumor*. (Indianapolis: The Bobbs-Merrill Company, 1966.)

[14] Goldberg, 2016.

[15] Rowe-McCulloch, Maris. (2019). Poison on the Lips of Children: Rumors and Reality in Discussions of the Holocaust in Rostov-on-Don (USSR) and Beyond. The Journal of Holocaust Research, 3393), 157-174.

[16] Byford, Jovan. (2010). "Shortly afterwards we heard the sound of the gas van": Survivor testimony and the Writing of History in Socialist Yugoslavia. History and Memory, 22(1), 5-47.

[17] Halbwachs, Maurice. On Collective Memory. (Lewis A. Coser, Editor, Translator.) (Chicago: The University of Chicago Press, 1992.)

[18] This biographical information was found in: Smith, Arthur L. Jr. *Die Hexe von Buchenwald*, (Weimar: Boehlau Verlag, 1995), and Whitlock, Flint. *The Beasts of Buchenwald*, (Wisconsin: Brule Publishing, 2011).

[19] For the sake of simplicity I have used the US equivalents for SS ranks.

[20] https://www.newspapers.com/browse/us/california/pasadena/metropolitan-pasadena-star-news_22568

[21] https://www.newspapers.com/browse/us/texas/mexia/the-mexia-weekly-herald_791

[22] INSPECTION OF GERMAN CONCENTRATION CAMP FOR POLITICAL PRISONERS LOCATED AT BUCHENWALD ON THE NORTH EDGE OF WEIMAR. Brigadier General Eric F. Wood, Lieutenant Coloenol Charles K. Ott, and Chief Warrant Officer S.M. Dye. April 25, 1945.

[23] This article appeared in many newspapers. One was The Brattleboro Reformer, of Brattleboro, VT, which ran the story on page 8.

[24] https://www.newspapers.com/browse/us/iowa/des-moines/des-moines-tribune_84

[25] This statement labeled with the following information: Mobile Field Interrogation Unit No. 2. PW Intelligence Bulletin. No. 2/20, 19 December 1944. Address Briefs and Requests to HQ, FID, MOS, APO 887. It is entitled, "SIX YEARS IN BUCHENWALD".

[26] Ibid., p. 6.

[27] This document is titled, "Testimony of ANDREAS PFAFFENBERGER, taken at Nurnberg, Germany on 1 February 1946, 1430-1530, by Thomas J. Dodd and Lt. Daniel F. Margolies. Also present: Hans Nathan; Bert Stein, Interpreter; and Anne Daniels, Court Reporter."

[28] Waldemar Hoven was an SS physician at Buchenwald; Martin Sommer was a notorious SS guard who was especially hated by the prisoners for his viciousness and cruelty; Hermann Florstedt was Karl Otto Koch's adjutant. There were rumors that Ilse Koch had extramarital relationships with Hoven and Florstedt.

[29] A letter from Liaison Detachment, Theater Judge Advocate, Office of the United States Chief of Counsel, APO 403, to Lt. Margolies dated 3 January 1946, includes the following statement: "Inclosed is a statement by Dr. Konrad Morgen who tried the Kochs. Other affidavits and statements by Morgen are *en route* by courier. It is suggested that if further information is desired Dr. Morgen may be brought to Nurnberg by contacting MIS at Oberursel." This letter also includes some information about the atrocity exhibits that had been entered into evidence: "The statements of Dr. Morgen bear to some extent upon the atrocity exhibits. In addition, I am advised that when Major Walsh picked up these exhibits, attached thereto were detailed affidavits with respect to their source. It is suggested that an effort be made to locate these affidavits in the OCC files" The letter was signed by Lt. Col Calvin A. Behle.

[30] Whitlock, Flint. The Beasts of Buchenwald. (Brule, WI: Cable Publishing, 2011). Pp. 123-126.

[31] Whitlock, *Beasts,* pp. 130-131.

[32] United States Holocaust Memorial Museum online encyclopedia, Lublin/Majdanek

Camps, https://encyclopedia.ushmm.org/content/en/article/lublin-majdanek-concentration-camp-conditions, retrieved November 29, 2020.

[33] "Great Escapes", http://www.majdanek.eu/en/news/escapes___episode_2__the_great_escape_from_kl_lublin/1220, retrieved November 29, 2020.

[34] From Konrad Morgen's signed statement dated 28 December, 1945 at Oberursel. "The discovery of the crimes of SS-Standartenfuhrer KOCH are due to a coincidence. Towards the end of June 1943, I received the order from the Reich criminal police office by request of the SS- and police court KASSEL to investigate the transgressions of a member by the name of BORNSCHEIN of the concentration camp at Buchenwald. Through this order I first obtained entrance into a concentration camp and there was confronted by the crimes of the Standartenfuhrer Koch and his headquarters staff." P. 3.

[35] Morgen had been sent to a Waffen-SS unit on the Russian front as a common soldier, perhaps in retaliation for his enthusiasm for prosecuting prominent SS figures. He was recalled from that duty in 1943 to handle the Koch case.

[36] Ibid., p. 1.

[37] See, for example, Elsner, Peter. (2017). "75 years after Erich Wagner's doctoral dissertation: "A Contribution to the Issue of Tattooing"—scientific misconduct in Nazi Germany. *Journal of the German Society of Dermatology*, 15(11), 1152-1154.

[38] Konrad Morgen statement, 28 December 1945, p. 2.

[39] *EIN BEITRAG ZUR TÄTOWIERUNGSFRAGE,* 1940 UNIVERSITY OF JENA DOCTORAL DISSERTATION ON TATTOOS BY SS-UNTERSTURMFÜHRER ERICH WAGNER, ASSISTANT DOCTOR OF RESERVES IN THE WAFFEN-SS.

[40] There is a record of a message at Buchenwald dated April 7, 1944, from SS-Colonel Lolling, Chief SS physician, to the chief physician at Buchenwald requesting that 142 pieces of

tattoos be sent to him immediately by courier.

[41] Hackett, David A. *The Buchenwald Report.* (Boulder: Westview Press, 1995).

[42] Kogon, Eugen. *Der SS-Staat: das System der Deutschen Konzentrationslager.* (Dusseldorf: Verlag L. Schwann, 1946). Also published in English as: Kogon, Eugen. *The Theory and Practice of Hell: The German Concentration Camps and the System behind Them.* (New York: Farrar, Strauss, and Giroux, 1950).

[43] Kurt Titz (sometimes spelled Dietz) was a kalfaktor in the home of the Kochs at Buchenwald. On one occasion he broke into the Koch's supply of alcohol when he alone in the house, got drunk, and vandalized the house and the personal property of Ilse Koch. He apparently broke up some crockery and tried on some of Ilse Koch's clothes, which were damaged in the process. He testified against Ilse Koch. It has seemed surprising to many that Titz lived to tell his tale, as his transgressions against Ilse Koch and her household were quite severe. If she was given to capricious acts of violence and incitement to murder with little or no provocation, how is it that Titz was not executed for this extreme provocation?

[44] Nobel nomination archive, https://www.nobelprize.org/nomination/archive/show_people.php?id=8684, retrieved 30 November 2020.

[45] Hilberg, Raul. *The Destruction of the European Jews: The Revised and Definitive Edition.* (New York: Holmes and Meier, 1985). p. 967.

[46] Herbert Marcuse, "Did Nazis use human body fat to make soap?", http://marcuse.faculty.history.ucsb.edu/dachau/legends/soap, retrieved January 13, 2021.

[47] I and J are quite similar in German script

[48] Neander, Joachim. (2006). The Danzig Soap Case: Facts and Legends around "Professor Spanner" and the Danzig Anatomic Institute 1944-1945. *German Studies Review,* 29(1), 63-86. p. 65

[49] Ibid., p 65.

[50] Ibid., p 66.

[51] Ibid., p. 66.

[52] Ibid., p. 66.

[53] Ibid., p. 66.

[54] Ibid., p. 67.

[55] Ibid., p. 67.

[56] Neander, *Danzig*, p. 75.

[57] Neander, *Danzig*, p. 75.

[58] Elizabeth Loftus, Creating False Memories, https://staff.washington.edu/eloftus/Articles/sciam.htm, retrieved January 16, 2021.

[59] Nuremberg Trial Proceedings, Volume 7. From the Yale Goldman Law Library, https://avalon.law.yale.edu/imt/02-19-46.asp, retrieved November 30, 2020.

[60] Whitlock, Beasts, P. 238.

[61] United States n. Josias Prince zu WALDECK et.al., Case No. 000-50-9, page 2.

[62] Whitlock, *Beasts*, Pp. 196-7.

[63] Newsweek, *Ilse Koch: Record of a Sadist*, July 28, 1947.

[64] Whitlock, *Beasts*, p. 235.

[65] The fact that there was a three-month delay in announcing the sentence reduction no doubt exacerbated its negative consequences. Some believed it had been deliberately withheld to avoid a predictably angry public reaction. The delay also meant that the news hit the newspapers just six weeks before the national election.

[66] Jewish Telegraphic Agency, "Senate Committee to Investigate Ilse Koch Commutation", http://pdfs.jta.org/1948/1948-09-29_225.pdf, retrieved 1 December 2020.

[67]Denson, William D. "I Prosecuted Ilse Koch", *The Gazette and Daily,* York, Pa., September 27, 1948, p. 17.

[68]There is a lengthy letter entitled "Second Trial of Ilse Koch" from the European Theater Judge Advocate General to Chief of the Civil Affairs Division, Special Staff, US Army, dated 29 November, 1948, which goes over the evidence against Ilse Koch that had and had not been used against her.

[69]Whitlock, *Beasts,* p 249.

[70]Jewish Telegraphic Agency, "Senate Committee to Investigate Ilse Koch Commutation", http://pdfs.jta.org/1948/1948-09-29_225.pdf, retrieved 1 December 2020.

[71]Allport and Postman, *Psychology,* 18-28.

[72]For example, in the Middlesboro (Kentucky) *Daily News,* under the title, "Did Frau Ilse Koch Order Tattooed prisoner Killed To Get Skin For Lampshade?", p. 4.

[73]Smith, Hexe, p. 177. "wenn Hitler wiederkaeme, wuerden viele ihm von neuem folgen"

[74]For example, in the *Portage Daily Register,* Portage, Wisconsin under the title, "Star Witness Against Nazi 'Red Witch' Now U.S researcher Into Cosmic Rays", on page 4.

[75]Whitlock, *Beasts,* p. 258.

[76]Smith, Hexe, p 203. "Ironischerweise waere Ilse zweifellos mit den anderen freigelassen worden, haette Clay nicht ihr Urteil geaendert und so Fergusons Eingreifen veranlasst was letzlich den deutschen Prozess nach sich sog."

[77]Hilton, Fern Overbey. (2004). *The Dachau Defendants. Life Stories from Testimony and Documents of the War Crimes Prosecutions.* Jefferson, North Carolina: Jefferson and Company. Pp. 143-156.

[78]I am indebted to my friend and colleague Connor Sebestyen for clarifying these points in a personal communication to me.

[79] JewishGen, https://www.jewishgen.org/ForgottenCamps/Camps/MainCampsEng.html, retrieved 1 December 2020.

[80] Drobnicki, John A., "Soap from Human Fat: The Case of Professor Spanner" (2018). *CUNY Academic Works*. https://academicworks.cuny.edu/yc_pubs/215, retrieved 1 December 2020.

[81] Ibid., p. 2.

[82] Ibid., p. 2.

[83] Her eye color was variously reported as green and blue.

[84] Smith, *Hexe*, p. 139. "Die Macht von Propaganda und Massensuggestion kann wohl kaum besser illustriert werden als im Fall Ilse Koch. Lange vor dem Prozess war sie in der Offentlichkeit schol als 'Hexe von Buchenwald'—als grunauegige, rothaarige, Nymphomanin, die sich daran erfreute, Lampenschirme und andere Gegenstaende zu Menschenhaut zu sammeln—verurteilt. Geschichten wurden begierig von Person zu Person verbreitet, die Presse schmueckte sie mit Grellen Details aus; jeder neue Bericht ergaenzte das Bild durch unwahrscheinlich Einzelheiten"

[85] Mastroianni, George R. Misremembering the *Holocaust: The Liberation of Buchenwald and the Limits of Memory*. (Colorado Springs, Colorado: 2019).

[86] Garry M, Manning CG, Loftus EF, Sherman SJ. Imagination inflation: Imagining a childhood event inflates confidence that it occurred. Psychonomic Bulletin Review. 1996 Jun;3(2):208-14.

[87] Schacter, Daniel L. (2002). *The Seven Sins of Memory: How The Mind Forgets and Remembers*. New York: Mariner Books.

[88] Werber, Jack. *Saving Children: Diary of a Buchenwald Survivor and Rescuer*. (New Brunswick, NJ: Transaction Publishers, 2014).

[89] Whitlock, *Beasts*, p. 203.

[90] Greene, *Justice*, p. 263.

[91] Werber, *Saving*, p. 41.

[92] Przyrembel, Alexandra. (2001). Transfixed by an Inage: Ilse Koch, the 'Kommandeuse of Buchenwald'". *German History*, 19(3), 369-399.

[93] *Newsweek*, July 28, 1947. *The Witch of Buchenwald: Record of a Sadist*. p. 38.

[94] Ibid., p. 38.

[95] Ibid., p. 39.

[96] Hartrich, Edwin C. The Evidence Against Ilse Koch. New York Herald Tribune, October 13, 1948.

[97] *Newsweek, Witch*, p. 39.

[98] Adorno, T. W., Frenkel-Brunswik, E., Levinson, D. J., & Sanford, R. N. (1950). The authoritarian personality. Harpers.

[99] Altemeyer, Bob (1981). *Right-wing Authoritarianism*. University of Manitoba Press.

[100] Though Spanner only ever admitted it was used in production of anatomical models, as a lubricant in the joints.

[101] Douglas, Lawrence. (1998). The Shrunken head of Buchenwald: Icons of Atrocity at Nuremberg. *Representations*, 63, pp. 39-64.

[102] Nemo, Charles V. (1956). *The Bitch of Buchenwald*. Male, 6(12), pp.32-35, 58, 60.

[103] Jacobson, Mark. *The Lampshade: A Holocaust Detective Story From Buchenwald to New Orleans*. (New York: Simon and Schuster, 2010).

[104] Harry Stein, Stimmt es, dass die SS im KZ Buchenwald Lampenschirme aus Menscenhaut anfertigen liess?, Buchenwald Gedenkstaette, https://www.buchenwald.de/en/1132/, retrieved 12/20/2020.

[105] Hackett, *Buchenwald*, p. 224.

106 Lorenz Schmuhl Diary, United States Holocaust Memorial Museum, https://collections.ushmm.org/search/catalog/irn505278#?rsc=184706&cv=0&c=0&m=0&s=0&xywh=-469%2C-164%2C3298%2C3277, retrieved 3 December 2020.

107 Ibid.

108 Schultz, Sigrid. "Makes Germans View Horrors of Death Factory". *Chicago Daily Tribune*, April 18, 1945, p. 7.

109 "Buchenwald Horror Still Haunts Sleep of Hoosier Warden", *The Indianapolis Star*, February 27, 1949, p. 22.

110 Ibid.

111 This appears to be visible around time-stamp 07:23. There is a dark area at what is the back of the lampshade in this shot which appears to be the missing top piece as seen in the Signal Corps photo.

112 "Tattooed-Skin Lamp Shades Said 'Missing', Times-News, Twin Falls Idaho, October 7, 1948.

113 "Tattooed Skin Lampshades Tagged as Evidence in Ilse Koch Case Disappear", *Schenectady Gazette*, October 7, 1948.

114 "Army Says Souvenir Hunters Have Evidence Against Koch", *Rome* (NY) *Daily Sentinel*, October 6, 1948.

115 "Human Head, Lamp Shade of Skin Are Shown as Evidence", *The Kingston* (NY) *Daily Freeman*, December 13, 1945.

116 "Army Says Souvenir Hunters Have Evidence Against Koch", *Rome Daily Sentinel*, October 6, 1948.

117 "Human Lampshades From Buchenwald Gone; May Be Some American's Souvenir". *Palladium-Item* (Richmond, Indiana), October 6, 1948.

[118] Bolling, Landrum. "Ex-Officer Has Human Skin From Ilse Koch's Home". *St Louis Post Dispatch*, October 3, 1948.

[119] Denson, William D., and Kunzig, Robert Lowe. "Why Should Ilse Koch Go Free?". *Look*, January 4, 1949, pp. 36-39.

[120] "Buchenwald Horror Still Haunts Sleep of Hoosier Warden", *St. Louis Post-Dispatch*, February 27, 1949

[121] Lange, Henry. "Buchenwald death still vivid to some". *The News-Dispatch*, Michigan City, Indiana, April 18, 1978.

[122] Ibid.

[123] Leen, Jeff. Ken Kipperman and the Table of Horrors. *The Washington Post*, June 24, 2001.

[124] Deutsche Ausruestungswerke—German Equipment Works

[125] Deutsche Erd- und Steinwerke—German Earth and Stone Works

[126] Gustloff operated factories at Buchenwald and also in Weimar which used inmate labor to produce small-arms and parts for the V-2 rocket.

[127] Zeiss produced optics for the German military.

[128] Look, *Why Should Ilse Koch Go Free*, p. 37.

[129] "Bonze" (pl. Bonzen) means something like "bigwig" in German. Many average Germans used this term to disparage officious Nazi functionaries, who were also sometimes called "golden pheasants" in response to their brown medal- and badge-bedecked uniforms.

[130] A translation of Erich Wagner's thesis on tattoos may be found among Lorenz Schmuhl's papers at the United States Holocaust Memorial Museum. Wagner reports (p. 44) that he studied 800 tattooed individuals at Buchenwald, with a total of 931 tattoos. Only three percent of these 800 persons were Jews, according to Wagner.

[131] Gilla Cremer, *Die Kommandeuse*, https://www.gillacremer.de/en/the-bitch-of-buchen-

wald-die-kommandeuse, retrieved December 12, 2020.

[132] Smith, Hexe, p. 203.

www.ingramcontent.com/pod-product-compliance
Lightning Source LLC
Chambersburg PA
CBHW072203100526
44589CB00015B/2350